Managing Electronic Resources

 Guide #20

Managing Electronic Resources

A LITA Guide

Edited by Ryan O. Weir

ALA TECHSOURCE

An imprint of the American Library Association

CHICAGO   2012

Illustration Credits: Figure 1.1 (E-journal Life Cycle) from Pesch, 2008. Image courtesy of Oliver Pesch, EBSCO Information Services. Figure 1.2 (Electronic Resources Life Cycle), adapted from Weir, 2010. Figure 3.1 (Bird-Fish-Animal Illustration) from DeLuca and Roach, 2010. Artwork by Roxann R. Reisdorf. Used by permission. Figure 6.3 (Session and Search Usage Trends of Web of Science before and after the Introduction of Substantial Full-Text Collections in 2009) from Web of Science® via the Thomson Reuters Web of Knowledge℠.

Printed in the United States of America

16 15 14 13 12   5 4 3 2 1

Extensive effort has gone into ensuring the reliability of the information in this book; however, the publisher makes no warranty, express or implied, with respect to the material contained herein. Readers should consult their organization's legal counsel before acting on any law-related advice from this book.

ISBNs: 978-1-55570-767-5 (paper); 978-1-55570-855-9 (PDF).

Library of Congress Cataloging-in-Publication Data
Managing electronic resources : a LITA guide / edited by Ryan Weir.
     pages   cm. — (LITA guide ; #20)
  Includes bibliographical references and index.
  ISBN 978-1-55570-767-5
  1. Libraries—Special collections—Electronic information resources. 2. Electronic information resources—Management. I. Weir, Ryan.
  Z692.C65M35 2012
  025.17'4—dc23
                                                                    2012015102
Book design in Berkeley and Avenir. Cover design by Rosie Holderby.

⊗ This paper meets the requirements of ANSI/NISO Z39.48-1992 (Permanence of Paper).

Contents

v

Contents

Illustrations

Figures

Tables

Preface

M any librarians find electronic resource management to be an especially challenging endeavor, both because electronic resources themselves are a constantly moving target and because most librarians have little education or professional development in the area. *Managing Electronic Resources: A LITA Guide* is designed to fill this void; it describes the basic strategies and concepts of electronic resources management, namely the electronic resources life cycle, and provides practical tools and strategies to prepare librarians to manage these e-resources collections.

Librarians have been engaged in managing electronic resources for more than 30 years, beginning with electronic databases in the 1970s; however, with the advent of the Internet came e-journals in the 1990s, and now e-books are fast challenging print books for primacy. The field of e-resources continues to evolve and change rapidly, and librarians must adapt and keep up with these new developments.

While the format and specific types of electronic resources and services that are acquired and managed within a library's electronic resources collection change quickly, the strategies and concepts discussed in this guide will help the reader face the ever-growing complexities of the field of electronic resources for the foreseeable future. When mastered, these concepts and strategies can be easily adapted and applied to new challenges and resource types that will inevitably be introduced to the field.

Managing Electronic Resources is composed of eight chapters written by librarians with a range of experiences from institutions across the country, all of whom deal with electronic resources management on a daily basis. The guide addresses the concepts and issues of electronic resources in a manner that is applicable to all types of libraries and institutions. Both seasoned electronic resource managers and less-experienced novices can gain helpful insights and strategies from this guide to implement in their libraries.

ORGANIZATION

Electronic resources, as with most library resources, have a life cycle comprised of multiple processes. The chapters that follow parallel each of the different processes associated with managing an electronic collection.

Chapter 1 introduces the field of electronic resource management. The focus is the electronic resources life cycle—the process involving the acquisition, accessibility, maintenance, and renewal of electronic resources. The chapter also gives readers tools to bridge the gaps that may exist in their own training and preparation for handling electronic collections. Suggestions are offered on ways to improve the knowledge base concerning electronic resource management, including sources to obtain additional insight and training. These strategies include: conference attendance, using online workshops and tutorials, networking, and monitoring electronic mailing lists. Armed with these strategies, any professional will gain a strong foundation for managing e-resources.

Budget challenges are the focus of chapter 2. This chapter introduces the reader to basic challenges a librarian may face at his or her institution and provides ideas and examples of both free and proprietary resources that will help the reader meet those challenges. The chapter discusses the issues surrounding stagnant or decreasing budgets and the options that libraries have to combat these issues. PDA (patron-driven acquisition), PPV (pay-per-view), consortial purchasing, and both proprietary and open source ERMSs (electronic resource management systems) products are a sampling of the concepts and products presented in this chapter.

Chapter 3 covers the discovery and acquisition of electronic resources, the first steps in the electronic resources life cycle. The chapter presents the basic skills needed to acquire electronic resources in a variety of formats. Topics include the use of ERMs, work flow, consortial purchasing, PDA, access and delivery, and a variety of other topics related to the successful acquisition of electronic collections.

Building on chapter 3, chapter 4 examines licensing and negotiating terms and pricing for electronic resources collections. The chapter begins with a discussion of the history of copyright law and contract law, as well as how copyright law and contract law differ. This difference is vitally important for every library professional working with licensing and electronic resources to understand, because electronic resources are not normally governed by copyright but rather the language that is negotiated in each license for each individual resource. The outcome of these negotiations will determine the freedom of use that the end user will or will not have with the resource. The chapter provides two main strategies for determination and organization of desired contract terms and desired terms checklists and for creating a model license.

After successfully purchasing and negotiating the content of the electronic resource, the next step in the e-resources life cycle is to make these resources available to patrons. Chapter 5 details myriad ways librarians can provide access to these e-resources to their patrons and gives insights about managing and troubleshooting this access during the subscribed access. After a brief discussion of access and security issues, the chapter focuses on eight different online access methods: online public access catalogs (OPACs), e-resources portals such as A–Z lists, subject indexes, federated search engines, link resolvers, discovery services, browsing lists (such as database and journal lists), and embedded lists.

Chapter 6 delves into gathering and evaluating usage statistics, which are needed to make purchasing decisions for the subsequent fiscal year, and how to communicate this information to all of the library's stakeholders. Effective and efficient gathering and dissemination of statistics is vital to support and advocate for electronic resources collections. This chapter also looks at usability issues of online resources and provides real-world insight and practical advice and solutions to statistics gathering and dissemination.

Electronic resources librarians and library managers will need to address a variety of concerns and issues that will surface that involve workload management between traditional print collections and electronic resources collections, including possible restructuring of existing staff. Chapter 7 details how to meet the needs of a dynamic electronic environment and how to be an organizational leader by offering the following strategies and discussions: managing up (managing interactions and information flow with superiors), supervising employees, coaching colleagues, creating and maintaining teams, using appreciative inquiry, backcasting, and training new and existing staff.

Finally, chapter 8 takes an informational and insightful look at what is coming down the road for electronic resources. Topics include how e-books may change libraries, access problems, electronic resources becoming the primary collection/

service of libraries, open access, library closures and consolidations, organizational change in libraries, changes in public services, changes in special collections and archives, the relationship between electronic resources and technical services units, the role of consortia, potential challenges, and the shift from collection development to information as a service. Through these discussions, the reader will gain a sense of where the profession and electronic resources field may be headed, including the potential challenges that may face libraries and electronic resources professionals in the future.

Electronic resources is truly an exciting and dynamic field that is continually changing. *Managing Electronic Resources* serves as a wide-ranging resource that will help the reader navigate these complexities. The guide not only provides the reader with an introductory look at the field of electronic resources today, but also introduces the reader to strategies and concept discussions that will enable any professional to effectively manage e-resources in the future. Managing electronic resources collections effectively and efficiently can make or break the modern library's acquisitions budget and collection development goals!

Chapter One

Learning the Basics of Electronic Resource Management

Ryan O. Weir

M anaging e-resources is vastly different from managing print legacy collections. While print collection management can at times be complicated, dealing with resources in electronic format adds additional layers of complexity to the process of managing collections. Electronic resources are ordered and invoiced much the same way as print materials, but there the similarities end. Electronic resources must be made available to patrons who are both physically in the library and those patrons who wish to access the materials remotely. The process of acquiring, licensing, troubleshooting, and providing access to these materials is complex and, in most cases, is developed over time once an individual has taken on the role of managing electronic collections. There are, however, ways an individual can seek to prepare before entering the profession and during the initial phases of employment.

Electronic resource management by its very nature is a dynamic and ever-changing field that has evolved from humble beginnings to a discipline that reaches into almost every aspect of the modern library collections. While electronic resources as a type of material format has been in existence for a long time, the professionals needed to address the complex variables of managing such collections have in many cases had to teach themselves what it takes to successfully manage these collections and thus are in a state of perpetual evolution. "Two decades after the advent of electronic journals and databases, librarians are still grappling with ways to best manage these resources in conjunction with their print resources. In addition, economic pressures at most institutions of higher learning are resulting

1

in librarians having to justify each dollar spent on collections and resource management" (Emery and Stone, 2011). This guide assists those professionals by offering practical insights and strategies to help them succeed in the realm of electronic resource management. Electronic resources collections differ from more traditional print collections due to the technology, price negotiation, contract negotiating, and access issues that are inherent in the resources' procurement and maintenance. All of these topics will be discussed in the various chapters of this guide. The main focuses of this chapter are a discussion of the basics of successfully managing an electronic resources collection, basic personal management skills and the concept discussions of the electronic resources life cycle. These focuses frame the additional concept and strategy discussions of the guide.

The complexities of the field of electronic resource management are further complicated by the wide range of types of electronic resources. The range of items now being offered in electronic format continues to grow on a yearly basis. Journals, books, datasets, databases, hybrid content, audiovisual files, and services continue to evolve into unique forms of electronic content, which in turn create an ever-growing complexity in the day-to-day professional lives of those individuals working with these collections. In addition, each of the formats may also be offered via multiple access and ownership options that influence the patron's ability to freely use and navigate these resources that must be taken into account every time an electronic resource is acquired. All of the following access models are discussed within the chapters of the guide:

> **Medical/Academic**
>
> "The transition from print to electronic resources has meant better service to library patrons and helps advance the research and patient care missions of the Yale University School of Medicine and its affiliated hospital. The challenges of managing electronic resources have forced library staff throughout the Yale University Library System to work together more collaboratively and have created a more cooperative work environment, but this work is still far from being centralized." (Dollar et al., 2007: 154)

- Traditional access model (ownership through contract)
- Access through pay-per-view services
- Database access
- Patron-driven acquisition
- Access to content through yearly subscription

A professional in the position of managing these collections must multitask, sometimes taking on many duties both in number and function simultaneously in order to be successful. These tasks can be easily managed when using effective time management strategies and scheduling/tracking tools. Many of these tools are also discussed throughout the chapters of this guide, ranging from Google Docs to proprietary ERM systems.

Even though this switch in

> ### K–12/Academic
>
> "The survey of school librarians extends what we know about the desirability of print reference sources at the K–12 level. Print reference resource use exhibits a general decline versus their electronic counterparts, receiving the least use at both higher education and school libraries. Although the preference for print reference resources increases as we move down from high schools to middle schools to elementary schools, in no case are print reference sources the preferred format." (Lanning and Turner, 2010: 218–219)

dominant format to electronic content adds several levels of complexity, the benefits to the end user (patron) far outweigh these changes. These benefits and user preference levels can be seen at libraries across the spectrum.

3

THE ELECTRONIC RESOURCES LIFE CYCLE

The electronic resources life cycle has become the standard concept by which electronic collections are acquired and managed. One of the best and earliest depictions of this cycle was featured in an article by Oliver Pesch (2008), "Library Standards and E-Resource Management: A Survey of Current Initiatives and Standards Efforts." Figure 1.1, the E-journal Life Cycle, shows Pesch's life cycle. His graphic walks the viewer through the stages of the e-journal life cycle. This guide will attempt to expand on this early concept and image to encompass the life cycles of all electronic content through discussions on the various tasks associated with acquiring and maintaining these resources.

Pesch's image can be applied to almost any resource within an electronic resources collection if slight variations are made to accommodate the difference in the resources. Electronic resources collections as a whole function within this same cycle; this is perhaps the most important concept that a professional must be familiar with when working with electronic resources collections. The cycle takes the resource from discovery to acquisition to renewal and back again, and is generally performed on a yearly basis. The process will be the same for most

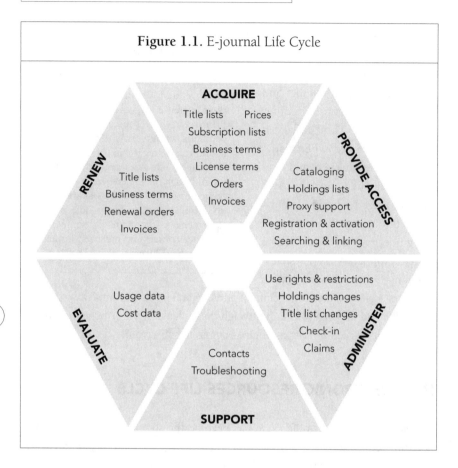

Figure 1.1. E-journal Life Cycle

resources within a collection, but may differ slightly from resource to resource. For example, a resource may be discovered by a librarian in one instance while researching new resources and be requested by a patron in another scenario. This guide loosely bases the format of its discussion on the concept of the electronic resources life cycle as depicted in figure 1.2. The stages of the cycle discussed are:

- Discovery of a resource
- Trial of a resource and quote request
- Acquisition of a resource / price negotiation
- Contract negotiation (licensing)
- Activation and provision of access
- Statistics gathering
- Troubleshooting
- Review and renewal of a resource

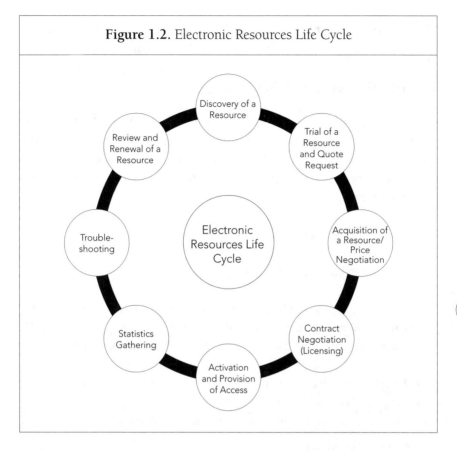

Figure 1.2. Electronic Resources Life Cycle

Discovery (Becoming Aware) of a New Potential Resource

A resource may be discovered in a variety of ways, such as a vendor sales call, e-mail, or brochure; a subject librarian referral; or a patron referral. The manner of discovery for each resource may vary greatly within an institutional organization, but will definitely vary even more between types of libraries. Regardless of the form in which the discovery takes place, the initial point of interest is only the beginning of the discovery process. Once a resource of interest is identified, the following items must be determined and assessed:

- Overlap with current content
- License terms
- Possible access points and issues
- Pricing
- Audience size

Many of these items can be determined through engaging the next step of the life cycle, the trial of the resource, and a provisional quote request.

Trial of a Resource and Quote Request

The quote and trial process for each library will need to be established within parameters that meet the need of each type of organization. At many organizations these two steps are managed by the electronic resources department and the acquisitions department. During the quote and trial process make sure to have the following information available:

- FTE or population served
- IP range
- Number and addresses of site(s)

When setting up a trial, a librarian needs to ensure that the trial is configured in a manner that will meet the information needs of evaluating the resource for potential use. The librarian will need to determine the following variables:

- Length of the trial (sometimes this is negotiable, sometimes not)
- Target audience
- Mode of access and authentication for the target audience

    IP authentication
    Log-in and password access

- Availability of the target audience: Certain times of the year, in many cases, are better than others for trialing new resources. For school and university libraries, this may be during the middle of the semesters when teachers and professors are not consumed with year-end grading or assignments. For public libraries this may be the summer months, when more patrons are available to use the resources in-house.
- How will the trial be evaluated?

    Statistical information provided by the vendor/publisher
    Patron feedback
    Other forms of feedback such as surveys or other online tools

- How will the patron feedback be solicited and gathered?

Once a determination has been made on whether the resource will be acquired, the resource moves into the category of a resource that will not be acquired or moves into the acquisitions phase. It is important to note here that pricing was requested at the time of the trial request. Proceeding in this manner will ensure that work is not put into resources for which the institution or organization does not have adequate funding.

Acquisition of Resource / Price Negotiation

During the acquisitions phase of the cycle, the librarian who manages the collections or other designee will begin the process of price and access level negotiation. The first step of this process is generally agreeing on what price will be paid for the resource at a given access level. The pricing of a resource is generally negotiable; even though the resource price was quoted in the discovery phase, it is not necessarily the price that will be paid once negotiation concludes. Maximizing the institutional or organizational financial resources ensures that this step of the process is always fully explored. For example, the librarian charged with conducting the price negotiation may offer to buy more content or commit to a longer time for a subscription in order to obtain better pricing. If the sales representative has reached the maximum discount that can be provided to the library, but this price is still too high, ask if the representative can communicate this to a supervisor to see if additional discounts can be offered from a management level.

Traditionally, the acquisition phase has focused primarily on ordering, receiving, and paying for published materials and services. These responsibilities have expanded within the context of the electronic resources collection. Librarians working with electronic resources must consider the following variables:

- Quantity
- Purchase type
- Costs
- Archival rights
- Vendor
- License terms

Once the decision is made that the library wishes to acquire an electronic resource, the task of negotiating the licensing and pricing of the resource begins. Chapter 3 discusses the acquisition of resources and the variety of variables that must be taken into account during the acquisitions phase of the electronic resources life cycle.

Contract Negotiation (Licensing)

Negotiating the contract terms goes hand in hand with the negotiation of pricing. Contract negotiation is a vital step in the process of obtaining an electronic resource, because the contract governs the use of the resource by the end user (the library patron). It is important that a librarian or other individual responsible for licensing review the terms in detail and negotiate for as much flexibility as possible for the end user. If the library negotiator does not secure the required flexibility, the resource will not be able to serve the purpose for which it was acquired. Chapter 4 of this guide is entirely devoted to this step in the process. Most vendors and publishers will negotiate terms with the library in a fair and equitable manner.

Successfully negotiating the license terms of an electronic resource is vital to provision of access to the end user of the resources in question. Chapter 4 discusses the differences between contract law and copyright law. This chapter gives the reader a better understanding of contract law and of how to succeed in negotiating for desired terms. Some of the tools discussed in the chapter are licensing checklists and model licenses; the chapter offers both examples of these tools and information on where to find additional examples.

Activation and Provision of Access

The majority of the electronic resources that are purchased by a library will need to be activated in some form or fashion. Many vendors and publishers provide tools to assist both in the registration of these materials and in the provision of access. A librarian will need to choose the mode of provision of access for all of the electronic resources that are acquired. This step of the process must be executed efficiently and effectively to ensure that the resource that has been purchased will perform its intended purpose. Making the resource available to the patron in as many locations and in as many ways possible will ensure that the resource is used by the largest percentage of the potential user population as possible. Chapter 5 discusses the provision of access to resources and varied ways in which access may be provided to the end user.

Troubleshooting Resources

Electronic resources, unlike their print counterparts, come with a variety of issues and problems that may or may not occur during the life of the resource. These problems can range from human entry errors in date range availability or IP range information to errors in the products themselves. It is important for a librarian to know what types of issues he or she can resolve and what types of issues must be delegated to either internal organization information technology professionals (IT) or external vendor or publisher-based IT professionals. There will be many problems and issues that librarians will be able to fix using the administration interfaces of their institutions' subscribed products, but many others will require the assistance of others. Chapter 5 discusses this topic in more detail.

Statistics Gathering

Statistics are vital in the evaluation of resources as they come up for renewal each year. Stakeholders always want to know that they are getting their money's worth out of a resource. Statistics can be used as a tool to justify the need for additional funding, or even in the battle to minimize financial cuts. There is a variety of services that can be purchased to aid in the gathering and processing of statistical information. However, many libraries of all types and sizes choose to create their own statistics-gathering models using a program such as Excel to gather and breakdown the usage information for various resources and resource sets. Chapter 6 discusses these topics in detail.

9

With shrinking library budgets it will become increasingly more important to be able to show the use and cost effectiveness of resources, and thus it is important for all libraries to have implemented some type of usage-data gathering and interpretation program. Chapter 6 also discusses the nature of usage statistics, the gathering of statistics, the validity of usage data, and the effective use of the data once it has been gathered.

Review and Renewal of Resource

Review of the resource is the final step in the electronic resources life cycle. This step results in the renewal of the resource for another year, a multiyear contract, or the cancellation of the resource. This is the final step of the yearly process for most electronic resources subscribed to by a library. This step of the process may be conducted by a single individual or by a group of stakeholders. Many libraries have created a committee of people who work on this type of decision-making process. In many cases all of the following people are included in such a committee:

- Electronic Resources Librarian
- Acquisitions Librarian
- Collection Development Librarian
- Collection Selectors
- Reference Librarian(s)
- Library Administrator(s)

Once this step of the process is complete, the life cycle begins again for the next year. This step is discussed in chapter 3 of this guide.

CHALLENGES AND CHANGES IN ELECTRONIC RESOURCES

Electronic resources is an evolving field that will inevitably continue to change at a rate of speed that most library professionals are not completely comfortable with. Many of the formats and services of the future will be driven by libraries and the end users themselves, while others will be driven by the perceptions of library vendors about what the library community needs to survive and thrive in the coming years. It will be important for libraries to continually evaluate whether new products and services that become available have been driven by the realities of the greater library community or by the perceptions of library vendors and suppliers. It will be equally important to maintain an open line of communication and feedback between these vendors and libraries to ensure that the perceptions and realities coincide. Many of the changes on the horizon include numerous issues discussed within the chapters of this guide, and some that are not.

Due to myriad factors, library budgets across the country either have become stagnant or have been on the decline for the past decade or more. It is becoming increasingly more important for librarians to come up with inventive ways to stretch the money that they have been allocated for collections, and to investigate new avenues of funding such as grant funding and philanthropic donations.

Likewise, it is becoming more necessary for libraries to come up with homegrown solutions to data gathering, tracking, and management to decrease the number of dollars being spent on proprietary services that accomplish these tasks and thus increase the amount of funding available for resources. Chapter 2 discusses many of these pressing issues and difficulties that are currently facing libraries today and endeavors to provide real-life examples of solutions for some of the issues discussed. Chapter 8 discusses the future of electronic resources, both the future challenges and potential future products and formats on the horizon.

Once a professional understands the basics of electronic resource management, the strategies that are needed to effectively manage an electronic resources collection, and the challenges that may be faced in the future, the next steps in becoming a more effective collection manager are to identify the holes in his or her training, find the means to eliminate these deficits, and seek additional guidance and information when required. The following section discusses options for meeting a librarian's professional training needs and ideas for making connections with other professionals to help solve the challenges faced in the collection management process. The guide addresses each of the steps in the process and minimizes the number of areas in which additional training will be needed.

11

GETTING STARTED IN ELECTRONIC RESOURCES

For many professionals across the nation, the training received in a Master of Library Science program or other formal education did not adequately prepare them for the role of managing electronic resources collections. Luckily, many places offer strategies, guidance, and training for those who are new to the profession.

Personal Management Skill Sets for Electronic Resources

Before moving the discussion of additional strategies, training, and guidance specific to electronic resource management, it is imperative for a professional who manages these collections to understand the basics of personal management. These skills are time management, management of communication, and management of information. Without mastering these skills, a librarian will not be able to find the time needed to perform all of the work associated with the electronic resources life cycle for his or her collection and maintain a current knowledge base about the profession. Librarians need to be organized, efficient, and able to communicate effectively across a range of constituencies in order to efficiently and effectively carry out the duties assigned to them. The reader will see these issues addressed in various ways throughout the content of this guide. After ensuring that these basic skills are in place, it is time to move on to the acquisition of the strategies and knowledge base directly related to electronic resource management.

Education and Professional Development

There are many different types of education and professional development that can be explored. The four main areas a new professional should look into are:

1. Formal education: While still working in an MLS program, classes related to electronic resources, management, electronic searching, contract law, collection development, and negotiation would all be helpful in preparing for an electronic resources position.
2. Continuing education: Many of the professional organizations of libraries, consortia, and even some vendors provide additional continuing education classes and training workshops for library staff and faculty. Some of these sessions are offered for a fee, while others may be free.
3. Vendor webinars: Most vendors will offer free webinars to help librarians learn the specifics of their database content and search features and capabilities, and for training on their administrative software. Webinars are helpful because they are live presentations via the Internet and thus facilitate real-time back-and-forth conversations and questions.
4. Vendor tutorials: Tutorials are prerecorded vendor instruction sessions. Tutorials are usually available on topics ranging from how to perform a successful search to how to gather statistics using an admin site.

Conferences

Many conferences are available to library staff and faculty that will facilitate a better understanding of the profession; allow the attendee to network, speak with vendors on the vendor floor during individual events scheduled by the vendor, or at a prescheduled one-on-one meeting; and keep up on what is going on in the profession. The following are three suggestions for readers who want to have a rewarding experience and learn a lot about electronic resources.

ER&L

ER&L (Electronic Resources and Libraries) is a conference designed to offer opportunities for communication and collaboration of information professionals and topics related to managing electronic resources. The conference is held in different locations around the country and generally lasts for three days. In her article "Keeping Current in Electronic Resources and Libraries," Mary Moore offers many insights about the ER&L conference, including many of the benefits of attending the conference. Moore states, "No other conference seemed to appeal to all individuals working to develop, deliver, and assess e-resources" (Moore, 2011: 265). For more information on ER&L, visit www.electroniclibrarian.com.

Charleston Conference

Charleston, as it is referred to by those attendees who have attended in past years, is a conference that started out primarily as an acquisitions librarian's conference. However, Charleston is now arguably one of the best conferences for any librarian to attend, due to the wide range of session topics covered on a yearly basis, not to mention the large vendor floor. Speaking as a multiyear attendee, the Charleston Conference offers sessions on a wide range of issues, including many that relate directly to electronic resource management. The conference is large enough to facilitate sessions and discussions on a large number of topics, but small enough to get to know your fellow professionals and to speak with vendors one-on-one, and the venue of Charleston is breathtaking and engaging. For more information on the Charleston Conference, visit www.katina.info/conference/.

LITA Forum

The Library and Information Technology Forum is an annual event held to facilitate networking and the sharing of ideas between professionals in the library community. Held in various locations around the country each year, the forum seeks to showcase some of the leading technologies in the field and give professionals ideas on how they may be able to implement these technologies in their home institutions. Like the LITA organization, the conference is highly respected in the library community. For more information on the LITA Forum, visit www.ala.org/lita/conferences/forum/2011/.

A large number of other conferences are also worth attending. These conferences range from small local gatherings, regional and state conferences like KLA (Kentucky Library Association), national association conferences such as ALA (American Library Association) and ARL (Association of Research Libraries), and large international conferences such as LILAC (Librarians' Information Literacy Annual Conference). This is in no way an all-inclusive list; the best advice for any professional when looking to choose a conference is to do the research and talk with peers who have attended specific conferences.

Electronic Mailing Lists

Electronic mailing lists are a great way to keep up with conversations going on within the library community. The following electronic mailing lists provide information and discussions, as well as job advertisements and information on current trends. While not all of the following relate directly to electronic resources, they will all assist a professional in this field.

LITA-L
LITA-L is a list sponsored by LITA, a subgroup of the American Library Association. It is a list dedicated to the discussion of issues related to library information technology. For more information on LITA-L and other ALA mailing lists, visit http://lists.ala.org/sympa/.

Liblicense
Liblicense is a mailing list hosted by Yale University Libraries that provides a discussion forum for issues relating to licensing library content. It is especially helpful when advice is needed on the wide-ranging issues that may arise when reviewing licensing for content. For more information, visit www.library.yale.edu/~llicense/.

SERIALST
SERIALST is a forum moderated by Birdie MacLennan of the University of Vermont that discusses serials related issues. This resource is a good place to start for questions relating to print and electronic journal content. For more information, visit www.uvm.edu/~bmaclenn/serialst.html.

ERIL-L
ERIL-L is a list hosted by Binghamton University that is devoted to the discussion of topics relating specifically to electronic resources. For more information, visit http://listserv.binghamton.edu/archives/eril-l.html.

AUTOCAT

AUTOCAT is an electronic mailing list hosted by Syracuse University that is devoted to the discussion of topics relating to the cataloging of resources in any format. This a great place to go if questions should arise about how to catalog an electronic resource. For more information, visit www.cwu.edu/~dcc/Autocat/AutocatFAQ-2.html.

Building a Network of Other Professionals

As the next tool, and final point of discussion for this section of the chapter, a new professional in the field of electronic resources needs to obtain a network of other professionals that he or she can go to when a second opinion is needed. There are many situations in which having a second voice or perspective is helpful. For instance, if a librarian is researching a new resource for implementation at his or her home library, it is always better to contact someone in the profession who has already implemented the resource. By asking questions and learning from another library's successes and failures, the selection and implementation of a new resource can go much more smoothly. There are many ways to establish these relationships, but some of the best are the options discussed just above this section: establishing relationships during the MLS experience, attending and presenting at conferences, and using electronic mailing lists to meet librarians who are working on the same issues and topics.

The discussion lists mentioned in the section are another way to ask professionals about these types of topics if you do not know anyone who has or is currently working on a current project. It is important to note that lists are established with guidelines and expected topics of discussion and may exclude messages if they do not meet the list-specific criteria.

SUMMARY

So where does this leave professionals who manage electronic resources? To be honest, there is too much to do and too little time to do everything they would like to do, but after reading this guide they will have tools to assist them no matter what the budget or other financial implications. This guide instructs electronic resources librarians or other professionals who manage electronic resources collections on how to achieve a balance and will give readers practical tools and insights to aid in managing collections and relationships. In addition, it also serves as a window into the life and functions of electronic resources librarians for those who work with, supervise, or aspire to be someone in that role.

REFERENCES

Dollar, Daniel M., John Gallagher, Janis Glover, Regina Kenny Marone, and Cynthia Crooker. 2007. "Realizing What's Essential: A Case Study on Integrating Electronic Journal Management into a Print-Centric Technical Services Department." *Journal of the Medical Library Association* 95, no. 2 (April): 147–155.

Emery, Jill, and Graham Stone. 2011. "'What Is TERMS?' TERMS: Techniques for ER Management." http://6terms.tumblr.com/post/9997650918/what-is-terms.

Lanning, Scott, and Ralph Turner. 2010. "Trends in Print vs. Electronic Use in School Libraries." *Reference Librarian* 51, no. 3: 212–221.

Moore, Mary. 2011. "Keeping Current with Electronic Resources and Libraries." *Journal of Electronic Resources in Medical Libraries* 8, no. 3 (July–September): 263–271.

Pesch, Oliver. 2008. "Library Standards and E-Resource Management: A Survey of Current Initiatives and Standards Efforts." *Serials Librarian* 55, no. 3: 481–486.

Chapter Two

Coping with Economic Issues and a Paradigm Shift in Collections

Regina Koury

Tough economic times have been a reality for libraries in the past, but in many ways libraries across the country are being asked to make unprecedented cuts to their holdings and/or operating budgets. Libraries of all types around the country are also dealing with the paradigm shift of print collections migrating to electronic collections. While print resources may or may not increase in price on a yearly basis, electronic resources, regardless of type, typically do. This shift has only served to exacerbate the stagnant or decreasing funding for library collections. This chapter examines ways that a librarian or other professional who works with electronic resources can minimize the loss of content when being asked to cut expenditures on a yearly basis. The authors draw on practical experience as well as review the relevant literature to give the reader insights and practical solutions to some of the funding issues facing libraries.

BACKGROUND

Ubiquitous access to electronic resources is considered a norm for library patrons, due to the efforts of libraries to make a patron's access both easy and seamless. Long gone are the days when library directors would question the necessity and advantages of purchasing electronic resources; the patrons of today's libraries are well versed in both the availability of electronic content and the knowledge that these electronic resources are easier and more efficient to use than their print counterparts (Curtis, 2005). Electronic journals and databases have been evolving rapidly since the 1990s, with electronic books starting to enter the realm of readily accepted formats in the 2000s. For instance, in 1995, only 115 e-journals existed (Hawthorne, 2008). In 2007, Johnson and Luther reported that approximately 60 percent of the 20,000 active peer-reviewed journals are available in electronic format. Online journals are popular with readers. Use of library-provided electronic journals exceeds the use of print journal content by a factor of at least 10, according to a University of California study performed in 2007 (Johnson and Luther, 2007).

Access to content anytime from anywhere, no simultaneous user restrictions, online ahead of print, easy search ability, and linking to cited materials are just some of the potential benefits of online resources. The demand for purchasing these electronic resources continues to grow, but library budgets on the whole are either flat-lined or decreasing. For instance, electronic materials expenditures in public libraries increased from 1.2 percent of total operating expenditures in fiscal year 2004 to 11.3 percent in fiscal year 2008 (Chute et al., 2006; Henderson et al., 2010). Association of Research Libraries (ARL) statistics for 2008–2009 indicated that electronic materials expenditures in ARL member libraries had grown sharply in the past decade in comparison to library materials expenditures overall. The average ARL library spent 56 percent of its materials budget on electronic resources; and 82 out of 124 ARL libraries reported that they spent more than 50 percent of their materials budget on electronic resources (Kyrillidou and Morris, 2011) (figure 2.1).

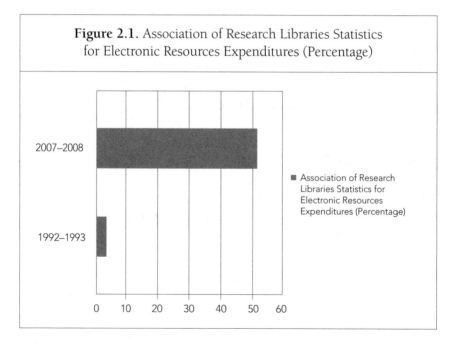

Figure 2.1. Association of Research Libraries Statistics for Electronic Resources Expenditures (Percentage)

Librarians are caught in a struggle between two equally motivating forces. On one hand, patrons have higher expectations for instant access to electronic resources; on the other hand, libraries have to deal with budget cuts and rising continuations pricing. Rising continuations pricing is a decades-long trend with no end in sight. While many publishers froze their pricing for 2010 (Annual Reviews, American Mathematical Society, Duke University Press), others continued increasing them at a 5 percent rate (Springer, Elsevier).

In addition, there have even been reports of publishers increasing their prices by up to 400 percent in some instances (Anderson, 2011). An announcement in February 2011 from HarperCollins, a publisher of electronic books, about limiting circulation of electronic books in public libraries to 26 times generated a huge uproar from library staff across the country (Hadro and Kelley, 2011). The circulation cap would force libraries, even with the discount rate, to pay for the same electronic book repeatedly each time they reached the circulation limit.

Managing electronic resources requires a complex and completely different skill set than that of managing print collections. In 2002 a survey on staffing for electronic resource management in libraries stated that academic libraries are in need of more staff to support the acquisition and management of digital resources (Duranceau, 2002). This survey backs up what those who deal with electronic resources have known for some time: as libraries continue to switch more and more resources to electronic format, staff time allocation must start to migrate away from management of print resources to that of electronic format. A quantitative analysis of full-time equivalent (FTE) staffing levels at academic libraries at 176 U.S. research universities between 2000 and 2008 showed that "overall staffing levels at these libraries declined but that the average number of professional librarian FTE positions modestly increased" (Stewart, 2010: 394).

THINK ABOUT THIS

Unlike print resources, electronic content includes many facets that have the potential to improve a library patron's reading experience. For instance, more and more publishers are offering new features for electronic resources, such as mobile interfaces, content suggestions, cross-search ability, and personalized search features for e-journals and databases. The American Chemical Society, Alexander Street Press, Gale, EBSCO, ProQuest, and Wilson Databases are just a few in the growing number of publishers that allow patrons to read peer-reviewed articles and keep up with the latest research on the go through mobile interfaces. Elsevier SciVerse is currently working on offering mobile apps for their content, and Gale has already developed an app for their electronic content collections.

The "2010 Top Ten Trends in Academic Libraries Report" by the Association of College and Research Libraries (ACRL) stated that libraries will have to step up to face budget challenges. Many libraries faced stagnant or reduced operating and materials budgets for the 2009–2010 fiscal year, and the near future will likely bring additional budget pressures. The average return for college and university endowments with minus 18.7 percent was in 2009, the worst year since 1974 (Blumenstyk, 2010). In addition, there is currently no federal stimulus money coming for 2012 budgets. The portion of state budgets allocated to public colleges and universities has been in decline for some time; the recession has exacerbated a trend whereby state spending on higher education failed to keep up with enrollment growth and inflation. Even when the economy improves, state revenues typically lag in their recovery by at least two years. All of these variables add up to a situation in which publicly funded academic institutions are seeing, and will most likely continue to see, yearly budget cuts (ACRL, 2010). The education cuts statistics are staggering. In 2011 the Center on Budget and Policy Priorities reported that 43 states implemented cuts in higher education. Colorado's funding was reduced by $62 million from FY 2010, Georgia cut state funding by $151 million, and $73 million was cut from higher education in Texas. The "2011 State of America's Libraries" report states that public libraries nationwide are straining from the effect of recurrent annual cuts in state funding, which offset the increases in less than a handful of states in fiscal 2011. Over the past four years, more than half the states have reported a decrease in funding, with cumulative cuts averaging greater than 10 percent (ALA, 2011). From the funding perspective, low or flat budgets affect both print and electronic resources collections.

FINDING, SAVING, PROTECTING, AND TRACKING FUNDING

The following is a collection of strategies and commentaries on how librarians may be able to address budget challenges while maintaining the integrity of their library's collection. With budget cuts and hiring freezes, chances are an electronic resources librarian will get to participate in e-resources evaluation, acquisition, license negotiating, data collection and analyzing, troubleshooting, cataloging, marketing, reference and instruction activities, setting up free trials, and maintaining vendor relations. Communication using free Web 2.0 resources and streamlining work flows are useful tools when meeting the challenges of all of these situations.

Reducing Journal Subscriptions with Aggregators

Canceling journals that are available through aggregators is one option for cutting subscriptions when there is no other alternative. Journal availability in aggregated databases is often subject to change on a frequent basis. Be sure to evaluate this option critically before pursuing it.

With budgets being cut across the nation, many libraries have recently been asked to create 5 percent, 10 percent, or 25 percent serials-cut scenarios. It seems that year after year library acquisitions and collection development departments compile journal lists and subject liaisons communicate with university faculty or other selectors to determine which journals can be considered for cancellation and which journals must be retained. As budgets tighten, libraries could consider cutting direct journal subscriptions that have been identified as low-use, and high-cost titles if they are available in the aggregated databases they license. This solution saves library money by eliminating duplicate payments for the same title, for example, canceling a print subscription to the periodical title *Broadcasting & Cable* because of online version availability from both EBSCO and ProQuest aggregators. Libraries that do this gamble that content for the titles will remain available and current; risk aside, they can generally count on continuous indexing for them (Thohira, Chambers, and Sprague, 2010). Among the risks are embargoes against current issues, publishers pulling content from aggregators, missing content or graphics in the aggregators, and lack of perpetual access if the library decides to cancel a particular aggregator (especially risky for state universities). Rick Anderson (2010) uses the term "the Churning Constant" to describe a publishing model that includes aggregator databases in which titles may change at unpredictable rates.

While there are many cons to canceling journal subscriptions based on their coverage through aggregators, for many libraries there are no alternatives to this strategy. With a majority of libraries already having fewer and fewer resources to consider for cancellation each year, this option is one that has been and is actively being considered around the country. Sadly, this trend seems to be repeated all over the country among libraries. The "2011 State of America's Libraries" report states that 19 out of 50 states cut state funding for public libraries from FY 2010 to FY 2011. Of these, more than half indicated that the cuts were greater than 10 percent (ALA, 2011).

> **FOOD FOR THOUGHT**
>
> Green Mountain Library Consortium, a consortium of libraries in Vermont, reported that in 2009 it had saved member libraries $2,440,354.

Performing an advanced search in Google for "collection budget and cuts" using ".edu" as a domain brings back results from numerous university library pages, announcing a new wave of journal cuts, spreadsheets for departments to choose which journal to cancel, and messages from library deans explaining the need to perform these cuts in collection.

Partnering with Consortia

Another way to save money is through partnering with consortia, if available. Orbis Cascade Alliance, GWLA, OhioLINK, LYRASIS, and GALILEO are just a few of the larger national or regional consortia that are available to libraries. Dan Tonkery, former vice president of business development for EBSCO, suggests using consortia for purchasing major electronic resources. He credits consortia with creating pricing models that allow subscription to all or most of the resources at a reduced cost. Libraries that historically have had print collections of 2,500 titles or fewer can now negotiate for access to major research collections at very little increase in cost (Tonkery, 2010). In 2011 Primary Research Group released *The Survey of Library Database Licensing Practices*, which reported that consortium contracts account for a mean of 43.72 percent of libraries' total licenses for electronic content (figure 2.2).

Elimination of Print Legacy Procedures

The idea of eliminating check-in, claiming, and binding has been controversial for years. However, savings can be generated using these ideas as well. Anderson and Zink (2003), early pioneers of this approach, reported that "one of the happiest

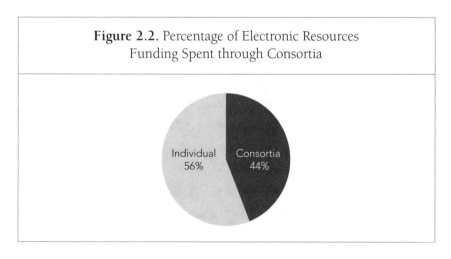

Figure 2.2. Percentage of Electronic Resources Funding Spent through Consortia

Individual 56%

Consortia 44%

consequences of eliminating check-in has been the increased speed with which new issues find their way into patrons' hands. The monetary savings from ceasing routine binding has been substantial. Binding was costing the main library roughly $20,000 per year; boxing costs less than $4,000" (p. 70) (figure 2.3).

Keep in mind that "one size does not fit all." Libraries that have implemented such a policy have done so to best meet the needs of their patrons and as a result of budget or staffing cuts or other pressing issues (Spagnolo et al., 2010). Murray State University is another example of this strategy. In 2008 University Libraries was spending approximately $35,000 per year on binding and related services. In 2010–2011, University Libraries spent $2,500 on boxes to box both new and existing unbound materials, and budgeted $7,000 for binding materials, of which only approximately $1,000 was spent on serials (figure 2.4).

Interlibrary Loan

Canceling journal subscriptions and relying on interlibrary loan for low-use, non-core materials to fill patrons' immediate research needs are other cost-saving ideas. Across the country, libraries such as the University of Arizona, University of North Carolina, and University of Washington "have already eliminated hundreds of journal subscriptions, with the expectation that user demand would have to be met via interlibrary loan" (Henderson and Bosch, 2010: 36). A cost-per-article analysis is

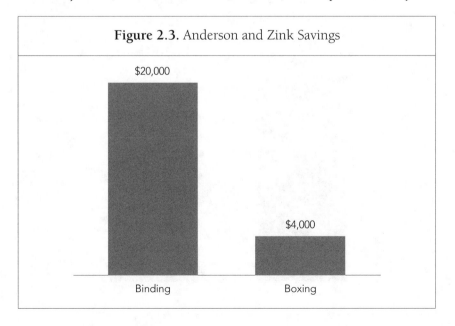

Figure 2.3. Anderson and Zink Savings

$20,000

$4,000

Binding

Boxing

helpful to determine whether an online journal subscription is worth keeping or canceling. An ARL ILL/DD Services Study performed in 2003 determined the average cost of borrowing transaction to be fewer $18.35 (Jackson, 2003). Canceling electronic journals whose cost exceeds $18 per full-text use or that are downloaded less than 50 times per year could be used as possible criteria sets for cancellation. Primary access health sciences libraries have been utilizing interlibrary loan to provide their users with access to important biomedical resources that are not available in their home libraries (Dudden et al., 2000).

Relying on interlibrary loan may cause a library to incur additional costs: increase in staffing to process requests and an increase in copyright fees for the articles exceeding copyright use guidelines, as well as delay for patrons accessing needed materials.

Pay-per-View Options

Pay-per-view (PPV) is another cost-saving alternative that many libraries are experimenting with. This option offers no perpetual access, but it provides articles more quickly than ILL for patron needs. Despite the concerns that have been raised about PPV, the literature contains recent accounts of libraries that have had positive experiences. Chamberlain and MacAlpine (2008), for example, describe

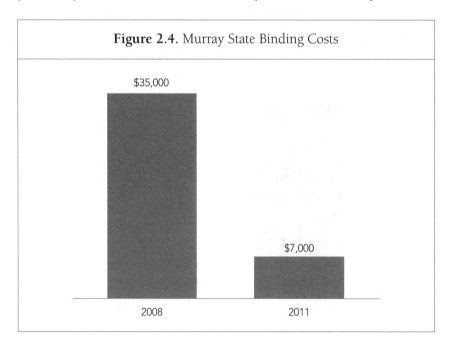

Figure 2.4. Murray State Binding Costs

$35,000

$7,000

2008   2011

the implementation of PPV at Trinity University. They report that in 2007 Trinity University decided to cancel all of its subscriptions to Elsevier journals and set up a PPV account. The account gives faculty members unmediated access to Elsevier journals, and students receive access to Elsevier journals pending the approval of a librarian or faculty member. In their conclusion, the authors state that, while it is too soon to make a full assessment, so far PPV has proven effective (Chamberlain and MacAlpine, 2008; Carr and Collins, 2009).

Not every publisher offers pay-per-view options for a large-scale PPV program. As of 2011, the list of those who currently offer large-scale PPV services includes Science Direct, American Chemical Society, and the American Physical Society. Many other publishers do offer PPV services in the form of credit card purchases from their websites, but these services are not easy to implement on a large scale in an academic setting. Overall, the PPV model, no matter its current limitations, allows libraries to offer expanded access to content for which they cannot afford traditional subscriptions (Weir and Ireland, 2010).

Another version of PPV is DeepDyve's rental program, which debuted at the end of 2009. DeepDyve offers several rental models, from one-day rental of an article for $3.99 to a $19.99 per month rental for 25 articles with unlimited viewing. MIT Press, Emerald Publishing Group Unlimited, and Association of Computing Machinery are just a few who joined DeepDyve in 2010. DeepDyve's agreements with publishers are limited and allow an option of rent or view only; however, they do provide a link back to the publisher to purchase and download the PDF.

At the end of 2011, another publisher, Cambridge Journals, announced a similar program to the DeepDyve Article Rental model: for a flat fee of $5.99, anyone can rent a view-only article. Before the patron enters payment information, Cambridge Journals has a note about possible access already available to the article via the patron's Institutional or Athens log-in. Cambridge Journals' rationale behind the pay-per-view model was the idea of improving access to research materials at a reduced cost.

Patron-Driven Acquisition (PDA)

With libraries worldwide facing reduced or flat budgets fight for physical space on university campuses and wider availability of online resources, patron-driven acquisition (PDA) has become a hot topic as an alternative to the conventional library acquisition of books. The idea of purchasing what patrons request has been around in various forms. For years libraries have used a "Suggest a Purchase" or "Purchase on Demand" acquisition model, whereby patrons have an option of requesting a book for a purchase through the interlibrary loan channels. The library would set up filters, for example, a price ceiling of $20 for the books to be purchased rather than borrowed, or purchase the book only if borrowing is not possible. In the late 1990s, NetLibrary, a book vendor, offered a patron-driven acquisition model. A model in which a patron's browsing and not librarian selection triggers the purchase of a book, allowing libraries to purchase content at the point of need instead of the just-in-case model of acquisition used by libraries since their inception. The original NetLibrary PDA model had several drawbacks, such as short trigger events for purchasing (short viewing times before purchase or limited preview options before a purchase was initiated), limited printing, and requiring patron registration for an account. In addition, low availability of e-book titles made this initial program unpopular.

In the 2000s, libraries and vendors are still working on developing better PDA program offerings. Currently, the process of setting up a PDA program follows several general guidelines. Library selectors initially work with a vendor (e.g., YBP, EBL, MyLibrary, Ebrary, NetLibrary) to set up a profile, followed by MARC e-book records loaded into the library's catalog for patrons to view. Patrons may view limited portions of an e-book for a short time, which is free. The purchasing process differs from vendor to vendor, from renting an e-book with the library paying a fee, to a library automatically purchasing the e-book and adding it to their collection after one to four rentals. PDA programs must be carefully mapped and controlled to ensure that libraries are not purchasing materials that are not going to be used and that purchasing does not exceed the funding available for the program. Many libraries across the nation have successfully implemented PDA. There are both pros and cons to PDA. One of the greatest advantages of a PDA program is that a library directs money for books that are used and does not spend money on books that are never checked out. E-books also save critical shelf space and offer full-text searching and 24/7 availability. The cons include lack of browsing and serendipity of finding e-books in an online version, which some patrons prefer. Also, not every subject is represented, and presently only a few publishers offer a PDA option. Some opponents of PDA raise concerns about "trusting" patrons to choose the right book for the collection, integrity of vendor-supplied MARC records, and whether this acquisition model is sustainable for all types of libraries. In 2010 the Publishers Communication Group conducted a survey of large academic institutions, which revealed that out of 250 libraries, 32 have PDA programs deployed, 42 have concrete plans to implement PDA within the next year, and an additional 90 plan to deploy a program within the next three years.

A 1979 University of Pittsburgh study on circulation and in-house use of books reported that 40 percent of monographs never circulated during the first six years after purchase. If a book does not circulate within the first six years, the chances of it ever circulating drop to 1 in 50. The trend is seen again in the recent 2010 Cornell University Libraries (CUL) "Report of the Collection Development Executive Task Force on Print Collection Usage," which showed that 55 percent of the print monographs purchased by CUL since 1990 have never circulated (Stewart, 2011). This is a staggering number, considering that in the time of the economic downturn, libraries have to choose carefully what to purchase or not.

COPING WITH A PARADIGM SHIFT

With an exponential growth of information, use of electronic journals, e-books, and databases will continue to grow. Library staff in charge of electronic resource management will need to continue to acquire new skills to stay ahead of the trends and provide seamless access to those resources. These librarians will be managing electronic resources using A–Z lists, electronic resource management systems (ERMSs), discovery layers, and federated searching and constantly readjusting work flow, staffing, and allocation of resources. A paradigm shift in the switch from print to electronic collections will retire certain work flows, like binding and checking in serials, and budget cuts will force many libraries to use creative ways to managing electronic resource collections.

Grants

Grants can fulfill the need for additional funding for increasing electronic resources costs. These materials typically increase in cost yearly, making it necessary to find modes of additional funding on a continual basis. By using connections within the university community, a librarian may be able to get faculty to actively include funding for library resources in their funding requests. Librarians know that the library and its resources are valuable to the continuing research on campuses. Many university departments realize that with budget cuts, library resources needed for their research may no longer be available. Educating and working closely with the university faculty can help you develop this avenue of funding. One downside to this type of funding for subscription-based products is that the life span of the grant will influence the length of access time to the resource. Be sure to weigh this and

27

other potential downsides before considering accepting or going after this type of funding for resources.

A librarian may wish to discuss this option with the grants office on campus, if such an entity exists. In most instances, partnering with the grants office will allow the library access to all of the active grant proposals and the majority of the faculty authors. While not all faculty can or will write in resource funding, this approach will allow the library to expand both their connections across campus and their potential grant funding opportunities.

Friends of the Library groups have been known to help public libraries with funding for collections and programming. For instance, East Brunswick Friends of the Library in New Jersey was recognized in 2010 by the United Way for its commitment to supporting library programs, services, and equipment. Specialty online databases are just some of the Friends' recent contributions to the library.

ERMS and Other Financial and Use-Tracking Systems

Another way for libraries to maximize their spending power is through data management and assessment. With the exponential growth of electronic resources and types of libraries acquiring them, the need for centralized management of those resources is paramount. An electronic resource management system (ERMS), is a tool that will track acquisition and renewal, licensing, and usage statistics without duplication. Managing electronic resources is a complex process, hence the need for an ERMS.

ERMSs have been in existence since 2004. In 2011 Collins and Grogg conducted a survey on desired features in an ERMS. Librarians' top ERMS priorities included work flow and communications management, license management, statistics management, administrative information storage, and acquisitions functionality. A single priority, interoperability across systems, may well affect all the rest. None of the available ERMS products, whether commercial (Serials Solutions, EBSCO, OCLC, Ex Libris, Innovative Interfaces, TDNet, Colorado Alliance, WT Cox, Swets, and Harrassowitz) or open-source homegrown (CORAL, ERMEs, CUFTS, and E-MATRIX), are able to address all of these features at this time. Choosing which ERMS to use depends on the size, goals, and budget of the institution. A 2007 ERMS survey on factors preventing libraries from acquiring a commercial ERMS conducted by Dalene Hawthorne and Jennifer Watson (2007) concluded that cost was the single-largest factor among libraries that do not have a commercial ERMS. Another factor to consider is that, in a tight budget economy that has libraries cutting collections, it is a challenge to justify purchasing a commercial ERMS. Homegrown ERMSs or Web 2.0 apps may be an alternative for the library with no budget money to spend. They do not require thousands of dollars in annual subscription fees, they are open source, and they are freely available to libraries worldwide for implementation, since they are usually developed and maintained by a library team. For instance, the Electronic Resources and Serials Access unit at the Hesburgh Libraries at the University of Notre Dame develops and maintains open-source homegrown ERMSs, CORAL and CUFTS. Another homegrown ERMS is developed and maintained by Simon Fraser University in Burnaby, British Columbia, Canada. Both of those systems are freely available to libraries worldwide for implementation. Because paying an annual subscription fee of $2,000–$15,000 or more for a commercial ERMS is not one of the cost-saving ideas, this chapter examines only the examples of homegrown, open-source ERMSs.

CORAL

CORAL (Centralized Online Resources Acquisitions and Licensing; http://erm .library.nd.edu/about.html), a homegrown ERMS from the University of Notre Dame developed by Ben Heet and Robin Malott, has licensing, usage statistics, resources (documents electronic resources work flow), authentication (can be used by institutions who do not have an existing authentication system), and organizations (names, addresses, and contact information of publishers and vendors) modules. It is licensed under GNU GPL Open Source license. CORAL modules may be implemented as part of the whole suite or as a stand-alone system. For instance, a library interested in managing license agreements only may install and use the CORAL Licensing module without the need to install the rest of the suite. CORAL has been made available as open-source software, is web-based, and was built using PHP 5 and MySQL 5. CORAL developers created a list with frequent updates and discussions to help with any questions or problems from libraries that are planning to install or have already installed CORAL.

Pros

- Free

- Interoperability within modules

- Users able to tweak any functionality

- Focuses on work flow process

Con

- No knowledge base; no integration with ILS or link resolver

ERMes from University of Wisconsin–La Crosse

ERMes (http://murphylibrary.uwlax.edu/erm/) was created in spring 2008 by William Doering, following the request from Galadriel Chilton to help manage the University of Wisconsin–La Crosse's electronic resources. As of November 2010, ERMes is used by nearly 51 libraries worldwide. ERMes is a Microsoft Access database that requires Access 2007 (Windows) or Access 2008 (Mac) to operate. ERMes includes renewal reports, year-to-date price comparison, cost per use per each database, and use report based on COUNTER DB1 statistics. It comes prepopulated with vendor names.

Pros

- Free

- Users able to tweak any functionality

- Ability to capture simultaneous user limits, authentication methods, subscription status, subject area or department affiliations, rights statements for ILL, document delivery, and e-reserves

- URL links to journal lists, license agreements, and user stats; tracking of database/vendor incidents such as downtime, missing content, and so on

- Availability of alternate log-in information for training access for patrons who are not yet in the authentication system or who are not able to gain access through the authentication system

- Hyperlinked A–Z list of databases for posting on a library webpage (Doering and Chilton, 2009)

Cons

- No robust knowledge base

- Not integrated with ILS or link resolver

CUFTS

Developed and maintained by Simon Fraser University in Burnaby, British Columbia, Canada, CUFTS (http://researcher.sfu.ca/cufts/) is one product in the reSearcher Open Source Software for Libraries suite of offerings. It provides basic electronic resource management services, allowing the library to centralize all of the details about electronic collections, including licensing terms, renewal dates, contacts, and more. CUFTS ERMS also features a renewal notification system that reminds of approaching deadlines, and an A–Z list of library electronic resources. CUFTS Journal Search tool allows a searcher to look up journal coverage in aggregators and dates of coverage, using the journal title or ISSN. Additionally, CUFTS Resource Comparison tool compares up to four databases at a time, providing quick analysis of serial titles and coverage dates in over 400 different electronic collections listed in CUFTS open knowledge base.

Pros

- Free

- Users able to tweak any feature

- Interoperates with knowledge base of 575 full-text resources, an integrated journal A–Z database, link resolving, and MARC records

- Provides e-book management for licensed packages, delivery of usage stats and cost-per-use analysis, overlap analysis, and fixed fields for license management

- Interacts with Innovative ILS (Simon Fraser's Library ILS)

Con

- Integration with Innovative ILS only

E-Matrix

E-Matrix (www.lib.ncsu.edu/e-matrix/functionality.html) is the locally developed serial and electronic resource management system at the North Carolina State University (NCSU) Libraries and is currently in use only at NCSU. It was built in Oracle and consists of three modules: service, interface, and synchronizer. The service module is the core of ERMS and was built using DLR ERMi data fields, which then were further customized. Some of the entities include resources, collections holdings, and licensing. The interface module is organized by the main entities from the service module, and access to each part of the interface is controlled by basic authentication/authorization. The synchronizer module consists of multiple synchronizers, filters, and transformers that load and maintain data in E-Matrix.

The E-Matrix licensing module acts as a centralized repository for all of the libraries' electronic resource license agreements. The module uses a mapping process to break each license down to its most important components, providing a staff view that is easier to read and interpret than the license agreement alone. E-Matrix populates the A–Z journal list, integrating holdings data from the Libraries' catalog and link resolver into a single format and allowing print and electronic holdings to be displayed side by side. E-Matrix holds local data, such as prices and usage statistics, and centralizes external measurements, such as impact factors. Any of these data sets can be combined, allowing advanced analysis on the basis of use, scholarly impact, price, and more.

Pro

- "Automated ingest and aggregation of data from both the ILS and the knowledge base. This means that staff don't have to transfer MARC records between the ILS and knowledge base in order to have data about print and electronic titles live side by side in staff and public interfaces." (Lynema, 2011: 30)

Con

- No open-source code to share with other libraries

Microsoft Access Database

Creating a Microsoft Access Database is an alternative answer to tracking electronic resource information if your university does not have a budget for implementing a commercial ERMS and/or your university does not have the staff to implement and maintain the homegrown versions. For example, Idaho State University (ISU) has been using Microsoft Access Database to track license terms, ILL and course packs restrictions, admin log information, and so forth.

INEXPENSIVE MARKETING

With the predominant change from print to electronic resources, the amount of marketing and information sharing that may need to be done when launching a large number of new or converted resources can become a challenge financially. In a recent survey, 9 out of 24 institutions reported no budget for these types of endeavors (Kennedy, 2011). So, what are ways to connect patrons with new electronic resources with little to no marketing money? Some of the strategies that have been implemented in libraries around the country are library newsletters, library instruction workshops, word of mouth, and advertisements on the library's homepage or via Facebook, Twitter, and text messaging.

State libraries and library associations created numerous tools for marketing electronic resources. For example, the State Library of North Carolina created Marketing Toolkit with examples from local public libraries, including key messages, coupon promotions, and stories from patrons.

Many universities throughout the United States have adopted Google Apps for Education. These free applications allow for ubiquitous access and collaboration and promote work behind managing electronic resources. For instance, Google Spreadsheets can be used to keep track of e-resources usage statistics. Google Spreadsheets allows librarians who are in charge of collecting usage statistics to share usage stats for electronic resources and collaborate with library liaisons and other stakeholders. In the past, the technical services departments at many libraries

Figure 2.5. Sharing Usage Statistics with Google Docs

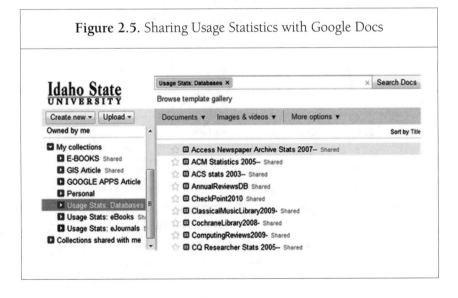

would collect usage reports, post them on the library shared drive or intranet, and provide them on demand from a subject liaison. With Google Docs, everyone can access those numbers and manipulate spreadsheets at their convenience. While Google Apps for Education are not available as a package to libraries not affiliated with an educational institution, most of these services are available to anyone with a Google account and therefore can be used in any library. Figure 2.5 is an example of how usage statistics can be displayed using Google Docs. For many institutions, Google Spreadsheets have proved to be more effective than using a shared drive in providing a transparent picture to many stakeholders at one time.

SUMMARY

The economic recession and the resulting decreased or flat budgets have pushed librarians to come up with creative ways to persevere and continue providing patrons with excellent customer service and better chosen resources. Many librarians have reevaluated collection development models, implementing pay-per-view and patron-driven acquisition ideas and relying on interlibrary loan to fill patron needs. Some other ways to face an uncertain financial future include partnering with library consortia for reduced rates on electronic resources, canceling "big deals," using open-source, freely available to libraries worldwide, homegrown ERMSs, and evaluating electronic resources using COUNTER usage statistics. While it is impossible to predict what the future holds, it is likely that librarians will continue collaborating with one another and with publishers on finding solutions to continue serving their patrons' needs.

REFERENCES

ACRL (Association of College and Research Libraries). 2010. "Top Ten Trends in Academic Libraries: A Review of the Current Literature." *College & Research Libraries News* 71, no. 6: 286–292.

ALA (American Library Association). 2011. "2011 State of the America's Libraries Report." *American Libraries*. http://ala.org/ala/newspresscenter/mediapresscenter/americaslibraries2011/state_of_americas_libraries_report_2011.pdf.

Anderson, Ivy. 2011. "Challenges to Licensing from Some Publishers." California Digital Library. www.cdlib.org/services/collections/current/challenges.html.

Anderson, Rick. 2010. "Managing Multiple Models of Publishing in Library Acquisitions." *Against the Grain* 22, no. 1: 18–20.

Anderson, Rick, and Steven D. Zink. 2003. "Implementing the Unthinkable: The Demise of Periodical Check-in at the University of Nevada." *Library Collections, Acquisitions, and Technical Services* 27, no. 1: 61–71.

Blumenstyk, Goldie. 2010. "Average Return on Endowment Investments Is Worst in Almost 40 Years." *Chronicle of Higher Education* 56 (January 28). http://chronicle.com/article/Average-Return-on-Endowment/63762/.

Carr, Patrick L, and Maria Collins. 2009. "Acquiring Articles through Unmediated, User-Initiated Pay-per-View Transactions: An Assessment of Current Practices." *Serials Review* 35, no. 4: 272–277.

Chamberlain, Clint, and Barbara MacAlpine. 2008. "Pay-per-View Article Access: A Viable Replacement for Subscriptions?" *Serials: The Journal for the Serials Community* 21, no. 1: 30–34.

Chute, A., P. E. Kroe, P. O'Shea, T. Craig, M. Freeman, L. Hardesty et al. 2006. "Public Libraries in the United States: Fiscal Year 2004 (NCES 2006–349)." U.S. Department of Education. Washington, DC: National Center for Education Statistics.

Collins, Maria, and Jill E. Grogg. 2011. "Building a Better ERMS." *Library Journal* 136, no. 4: 22–28.

Curtis, Donnelyn. 2005. *E-journals: A How-To-Do-It Manual for Building, Managing, and Supporting Electronic Journal Collections.* New York: Neal-Schuman.

Doering, William, and Galadriel Chilton. 2009. "ERMes: Open Source Simplicity for Your E-resource Management." *Computers in Libraries* 29, no. 8: 20–24.

Dudden, R. F., S. Coldren, J. E. Condon, S. Katsh, C. M. Reiter, and P. L. Roth. 2000. "Interlibrary Loan in Primary Access Libraries: Challenging the Traditional View." *Bulletin of Medical Library Association*, 88, no. 4 (October): 303–313.

Duranceau, E. 2002. "Staffing for Electronic Resource Management." *Serials Review* 28, no. 4: 316–320.

Hadro, J., and M. Kelley. 2011. "HarperCollins: 26-Loan Cap on Library Ebooks." *Library Journal* 136, no. 6: 16–18.

Hawthorne, Dalene. 2008. "History of Electronic Resources." In *Electronic Resource Management in Libraries: Research and Practice,* edited by Holly Yu and Scott Breivold, 1–15. Hershey, PA: IGI Global.

Hawthorne, Dalene, and Jennifer Watson. 2007. "Electronic Resource Management Systems: Alternative Solutions." Paper presented at 73rd IFLA General Conference and Council, Cape Town, South Africa, August 16, 2007.

Henderson, E., K. Miller, T. Craig., S. Dorinski, M. Freeman., N. Isaac et al. 2010. *Public Libraries Survey: Fiscal Year 2008 (IMLS-2010–PLS-02).* Washington, DC: Institute of Museum and Library Services.

Henderson, Kittie S., and Stephen Bosch. 2010. "Seeking the New Normal." *Library Journal* 135, no. 7: 36–40.

Jackson, Mary. 2003. "Assessing ILL/DD Services Study: Initial Observations." ARL Bimonthly Report. www.arl.org/bm~doc/illdd.pdf.

Johnson, Richard K, and Judy Luther. 2007. "The E-only Tipping Point for Journals." Association of Research of Libraries. http://eprints.rclis.org/bitstream/10760/11127/1/Electronic_Transition_final.pdf.

Kennedy, Marie. 2011. "What Are We Really Doing to Market Electronic Resources?" *Library Management* 32, no. 3: 144–158.

Kyrillidou, Martha, and Shaneka Morris. 2011. "ARL Statistics 2008–2009." www.arl.org/bm~doc/arlstat09.pdf.

Lynema, Emily. 2011. "Q&A: E-Matrix and E-resource Management." *Library Journal* 136, no. 4: 20.

Primary Research Group. *The Survey of Library Database Licensing Practices*, 2011 ed. www.primaryresearch.org/publications.php.

Spagnolo, Lisa, Buddy Pennington, Kathy Carter, and Sharon Dyas-Correia. 2010. "Serials Management Transitions in Turbulent Times." *Serials Review* 36, no. 3: 161–166.

Stewart, Christopher. 2010. "Half Empty or Half Full? Staffing Trends in Academic Libraries at U.S. Research Universities, 2000–2008." *Journal of Academic Librarianship* 36, no. 5: 394–400.

———. 2011. "METRICS: The Next Chapter: Measuring the Pace of Change for Print Monograph Collections." *Journal of Academic Librarianship* 37, no. 4: 355–357.

Thohira, Mariyam, Mary Beth Chambers, and Nancy Sprague. 2010. "Full-Text Databases: A Case Study Revisited a Decade Later." *Serials Review* 36, no. 3: 152–160.

Tonkery, Dan. 2010. "Reflections on Forty Years of Serials Work and My Prediction for the Future of Our Industry." *Serials Review* 36, no. 3: 135–137.

Weir, Ryan, and Ashley Ireland. 2010. "Getting our Feet Wet: Library's Experience with Transactional Access." *Against the Grain* 21, no. 6: 16–20.

Chapter Three

Acquiring Electronic Resources

Denise Pan

I n 2007 the journal *The Acquisition Librarian* was renamed the *Journal of Electronic Resources Librarianship*. According to the editor, Bonnie Tijerina (2008), the title change was appropriate:

> Libraries are acquiring increasingly larger amounts of electronic format materials in this digital age. The collection, acquisition, and maintenance of these resources can be complicated, requiring organizations to think differently about management and delivery. . . . The development of this journal will encourage a more focused and critical examination of the digital environment's impact on collecting, acquiring, and making accessible library materials for today and the future. (p. 1)

In this context, it is difficult to identify or describe acquisitions as a discrete department that exists in isolation from other units. Traditional views of librarianship may assume that acquisitions functions are a subset of collection development or technical services. However, this may not be the existing reality when so much is in transition—economic instability, tight budgets, staffing reductions, new electronic formats and technology, and makeshift work flows. Essentially, each library makes personnel decisions based on their own situation.

Customary library organizational hierarchies are unresponsive to the dynamic nature of online resources. A horizontal structure could be more adaptive, yet it is not the current norm. Furthermore, the emphasis on electronic materials may be more evident in academic libraries, but it is an increasing concern for public and school libraries. Su (2007: 1) states, "Although the probability of a paperless library remains debatable, electronic material has become an inevitable issue to deal with for all the librarians in general, and for the acquisitions and collection development librarians in particular." For these reasons, this chapter describes acquisitions as a phase of work that initiates and facilitates the access and discovery of electronic materials, instead of as a specific department or position.

Moreover, conventional perceptions assume that commercial electronic resource management systems (ERMSs) are the solution to most problems with online materials. Despite these promises, most libraries using these systems "have achieved varying degrees of success in implementation and maintenance" (Kerr, 2010: 297). Undoubtedly, these systems can help centralize e-resource data regarding trial, usage, cost, access, and administration. Populating the knowledge base and changing established procedures, however, are often described as some of the major obstacles with ERMSs. While this chapter recognizes the value of various ERMS features, the focus is on describing acquisitions in the larger context of electronic resource management processes and procedures.

The fundamental work flow for all new library materials is to select, order, receive/access, pay, catalog, and assess. Depending on volume, all of these roles and responsibilities could be assigned to an individual or a team. As the quantity of new items grows and the variety of formats increases, ideally the staff size will expand to meet the volume and complexity of work. Selecting and ordering duties may or may not be combined and integrated with other responsibilities included in the subsequent work flow. Regardless of how work is delegated, decisions must be communicated throughout the process. These roles could be assigned to a librarian or clerical staff, contingent on the library. For consistency, this chapter assumes that all ordering, receiving, and payment functions are assigned to a librarian. To illustrate how these activities integrate with the selection-to-assessment work flow, this chapter provides an overview of issues that the librarian should consider when beginning and maintaining the acquisitions process. Specifically, they will learn how to categorize selected materials into a work flow framework, understand and document costs, identify the vendor, and facilitate access and discovery.

RECOGNIZING WORK FLOW FRAMEWORK

It is always helpful to participate in the trial, selection, and decision-making process. However, if background information on the new resource is unknown, before ordering the librarian should begin to ask questions that define the purchase and renewal procedures. Some basic queries include:

- What is the library purchasing? Is it a single item or collection of titles?
- How much will it cost, initially and ongoing?
- Who are the vendors?
- Where can it be accessed and discovered, today and in the future?

Once the decisions have been made, the setup process can take days, weeks, or months and involve myriad individuals with a variety of skill sets and responsibilities.

In the traditional print world, the processes are primarily defined by the physical format and frequency, such as monograph, video, audio, journal, standing order, and continuation. For electronic resources, the procedures are characterized by an entirely different vocabulary. Once the purchasing decision has been made, librarians are more concerned with identifying quantity, funding source, vendor, access, and ease of location (discovery) of the library material, rather than classifying the purchased content. Quite often a resource may be labeled as a "dictionary" or an "encyclopedia," but the online interface, authentication, licensing terms, and subscription period are the same parameters used to describe a "database" or other electronic resources. In theory, each type of electronic resource should include specific characteristics that would define its classification and appropriate work flow. However, the reality includes more exceptions than imagined, and each purchase can be a discovery of a new kind of "animal." To start, the librarian needs to categorize and quantify what is being purchased.

At the 2010 Electronic Resources & Libraries conference, Carolyn DeLuca and Dani Roach introduced attendees to the "Wild Kingdom" of electronic resources. They assigned a species to each type of resource (e-book, e-journal, and e-resource) and identified the common traits (see table 3.1). While they could name a title that represented a typical resource, they also found other examples with hybrid traits. The *International Dictionary of Company Histories* was classified as bird-fish-animal (see figure 3.1) because it is "published in both print and online formats; cataloged as multipart monograph; published in volumes; purchased with serial funds; and

39

[they] create[d] a federated search across all volumes and add[ed] new volumes regularly" (DeLuca and Roach, 2010). DeLuca and Roach's example and table 3.1 illustrate that the definition of online materials may also include physical/virtual format, content type, publication frequency, funding source, purchase type, vendor, archival rights, and licensing terms.

In addition to categorizing the online material into a relevant framework, it is also necessary to identify the quantity. Since libraries began purchasing article databases comprising of thousands of journals, the phrase "bulk buying" has new connotations for librarians. Electronic resources can include a collection of many online books, journals, proceedings, videos, sound recordings, and so forth. Some librarians are responsible for receiving purchased materials. Therefore, for items with perpetual access, the title and holdings lists can be viewed as an online packing slip. Stemper and Barribeau (2006) define e-journal perpetual access as "the right to permanently access licensed materials paid for during the period of a license agreement (not to be confused with the right to copy journal content solely for preservation purposes)" (p. 91). The librarian should verify the receipt of all goods. If staffing is limited, it may not be feasible to verify availability of perpetual access or purchased journal collections with thousands of titles. Since the content of aggregator databases is subscribed or leased with no perpetual access and titles

Table 3.1. Wild Kingdom of Electronic Resources

Bird (e-book)	Fish (e-journal)	Animal (e-resource)
• Monograph • Book $ • One-time purchase • Purchase options vary—vendor, direct, third party • May have annual subscription or hosting costs (but unlikely) • Licensing varies—from minimal to extensive	• Serial • Journal $ • By subscription • Purchase option norm is via agent • May have one-time archive or perpetual rights fees • License by publisher	• Integrating resource • Web resource $ • By subscription • Purchase options include consortium, direct • May have one-time upfront archive or perpetual rights fees • Extensive licensing

Source: DeLuca and Roach, 2010. Used by permission.

may come and go with the ebb and flow of the tide, confirming access to the resource should suffice.

Purchasing an entire collection of online materials may be cost prohibitive. A library may choose instead to order a single item or the same title in different formats. For example, most book jobbers, such as Yankee Book Peddler or Coutts, offer services for ordering individual e-books. The purchase decision can be made by library selectors or patrons based on profiles. Replicating established print book work flow can offer optimum efficiency. By choosing and ordering from the book vendor's system, librarians can leverage existing or create new profiles—a summary of purchasing preferences in terms of subject area, call number, publisher, price, and other criteria. The book jobber alerts librarians with slip notices on the latest and most relevant titles and provides brief bibliographic details, price, and access model. With this information the selectors can decide to opt in on the purchase. Unlike with an approval plan, the e-book is automatically purchased according to profile and the librarian has a limited amount of time to opt out of the order.

Figure 3.1. Bird-Fish-Animal Illustration

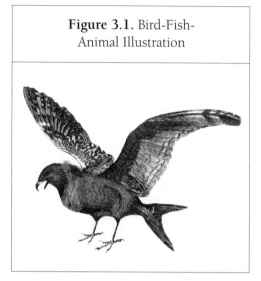

41

As budgets shrink and demand grows, libraries are increasingly interested in patron-driven acquisitions (PDAs). As Miller (2011) explains, "Given the volume of publishing that still proliferates, no library can be truly comprehensive, or afford to buy everything its users might want, 'just in case,' even with extensive funding" (p. 2). Libraries typically work with e-book vendors or aggregators to establish PDA profiles. The vendor supplies MARC records for titles that meet the criteria, and the library loads the records into the catalog. Patrons are given full-text access to the e-book when they discover the PDA title. Once the patron triggers the negotiated number of "uses"—often defined by views, printed pages, or downloads—the library is invoiced for the purchase or short-term loan. In this purchasing model, user needs are fulfilled "just-in-time" (Delquie and Tucker, 2011: 24).

UNDERSTANDING AND DOCUMENTING COSTS

Before ordering, it is best to double-check and verify that funds are available for the purchase, especially at the end of the fiscal year. Is it an expected or planned acquisition? Which fund account will be used to pay the invoice? Will the current allocation cover the expenditure? Considering the answers to these questions, it may be necessary to reallocate monies to the appropriate account or to cancel a subscription in order to purchase a new acquisition. If the library uses the acquisitions module of their integrated library management system (ILMS), they will create an order record at the point of purchase. This order record is attached to a bibliographic record and will include various details, such as categorizing the resource to comply with procurement rules, report on expenditure statistics to external organizations, and plan for future budget years. Libraries can customize the order record to capture this information in a fixed-length field (e.g., fund) or a variable-length field (e.g., note).

42

Depending on the organization's procurement, auditing, and risk management policies, identifying and reporting capital electronic resource expenditures may be required. Therefore, it is helpful to classify capital and noncapital expenses at the point of purchase. Capital online library material designation is generally determined by perpetual rights ownership; in the print world, when a library bought a book or subscribed to a journal, they "owned" a physical copy of that resource. Libraries had the authority to lend their collection to students or another library. Libraries no longer can assume ownership and the permission to lend or borrow purchased electronic content. Today, most e-resource acquisition requires a license agreement that will distinguish between leased versus perpetual access (see more details in chapter 4). Aggregator databases offer great quantity for an economical price. However, libraries pay a premium to maintain ongoing ownership rights to library materials (Stemper and Barribeau, 2006). If the content can only be accessed while the renewal or subscription is maintained, then it is often characterized as a noncapital expense.

At the point of purchase, understanding and documenting ongoing and future costs associated with the purchase will help during annual budget reviews. Renewals are most commonly associated with subscriptions to serials, such as journals. However, some online content previously envisioned as "one-time purchases," such as e-books, are becoming continuing expenses. For instance, new editions of online reference books are sold annually in a package. Maintaining the most current versions will require recurring orders, or renewals. In addition, the library may be required to pay fees to access or host the resource on the publisher's website, or to load and maintain the data locally. Stemper and Barribeau (2006) explain: "Either way (whether a library is paying the publisher or library or technology vendor support staff), sometimes multiple and ongoing costs for perpetual access will exist" (p. 99). Annual charges vary by publishers but can be generalized into three categories:

- Pay-per-title
- Maximum or flat fee
- Waive charge for current customers maintaining subscriptions to other collections

Regardless of the payment model, the librarian should plan for the possibility.

Predicting renewal pricing is guesswork at best. According to the *Library Journal* "2010 Periodicals Price Survey" by Kittie S. Henderson and Stephen Bosch (2010), "the average overall price increases for periodical subscriptions dropped from 7.6 percent in 2009 to 4.4 percent in 2010" (p. 37). Will future prices increase, decline, or remain stable? Only time will tell. In the meantime, the survey reported that "in planning for 2011 and beyond, managers are encouraged to use the traditional 6 percent to 8 percent inflation rate as a guide, adjusting the numbers based on the components of their distinct holdings" (Henderson and Bosch, 2010: 40). Estimating an individual library's price increases in the context of industry trends takes time.

For now, when budgets are tight and cancellations might be required, libraries may find it useful to request renewal quotes several months before the subscription period expires because the license agreement may require a termination notice several months in advance. To do so, some ERMSs, such as Innovative Interfaces' Millennium Electronic Resource Management, enable librarians to set up "ticklers" or e-mail reminders scheduled to be sent on a particular date. If no ERMS is available, most acquisitions modules of an ILMS will permit a librarian to customize a fixed-length field in an order record. The field can be assigned a number or letter value to represent the month the subscription ends or the renewal quote should be requested. Monthly procedures can be established to run a list of electronic resources based on the renewal month. Even a spreadsheet that lists the subscription period and renewal month can be a practical tool. Both the ERMS and the ILMS should be able to export a Microsoft Excel or a CSV (comma-separated values or comma delimited) file. Table 3.2 provides a hypothetical example of possible headers for an electronic resources renewal list.

Table 3.2. Hypothetical Electronic Resources Renewal List

Electronic Resource	Order Record #	Fund	Renewal Month	Vendor	Previous FY Price	% Price Increase	Current FY Price
Chemistry Journals	.01234	Journals-Cap-Chemistry	December	Chemistry Publisher	$10,000	7.0	$10,700
Reference Books	.02345	Books-Cap-Reference	January	Reference Book Publisher	$3,000	7.0	$3,210
Business Journals	.03456	Journals-NonCap-Business	January	Aggregator Vendor	$5,000	7.0	$5,350

IDENTIFYING THE VENDOR AND PAYMENT

Identifying the vendor and nature of the relationship can help expedite the purchasing process. Have there been any previous purchases? Is the vendor's information in the ILMS and Accounting system? What is the preferred payment method? Is a license agreement required? Knowing the answers to these questions can be very beneficial.

If the vendor is new and has no previous contact with the organization, then additional paperwork may be required. For example, a public higher education institution has nonprofit status and is exempt for federal excise taxes and state and local government sales and use taxes. According to the IRS.gov website, to exclude sales tax, the vendor may require a copy of the city, county, and state tax exempt certificates, and/or 501(c)(3) status letter from the U.S. Department of Treasury Internal Revenue Service (IRS, 2011b). Conversely, the librarian's institution may require a form to establish a vendor account in the procurement system and the federal requirement to request a W-9 or Tax Identification Number (TIN) in order to make payments for goods and services (IRS, 2011a). Have copies of certificates, letters, and forms readily available, as appropriate, to make the process as efficient as possible. For more information, the librarian should consult his or her institutional or organizational procurement offices.

With existing vendors, there may be additional opportunities to negotiate price. Some discount possibilities might include the following:

- Previous orders
- Multiyear commitments
- Access or hosting fees waived
- Multiple sites/campuses
- Agent or consortium purchase

However, unless the vendors offer more savings, the librarian should ask if returning customers qualify for any additional discounts.

Once the cost has been finalized, the next step is to ascertain the payment method. Most libraries can purchase materials with a credit card or authorize an invoice to be paid by the institution's accounting, accounts payable, or procurement department. Some organizations may need additional approvals before providing payment, such as requiring an internal purchasing agent to issue a purchase order (PO). Once the vendor account is established, invoices are efficient to manage since they can be processed to be paid quickly in the institution's accounting system and the library management system. Paying by credit card may be faster in the short-term because the vendor account setup process could be bypassed. The time savings might be moot if charges need to be verified against credit card statements, in addition to reconciling library and accounting systems. Nevertheless, payment method may be determined by the means in which the vendor accepts reimbursement.

Based on the organization's procurement rules, it may be essential to know whether a license agreement is required prior to submitting an order. Terms and conditions should be negotiated in advance of receiving an invoice or items. If both parties cannot reach mutual understanding, then no goods or services can be purchased. Negotiating terms after items have been ordered and received is often called an "after the fact" (ATF), which may be considered a violation of the institution's fiscal rules. Authority to negotiate licenses may reside inside or outside the library, such as the acquisitions department or university procurement.

Prior to the purchasing process, the librarian will want to know the internal policies for licenses and the vendor's requirements. For previously unused vendors who require a license, the agreement will be a new license. Existing sellers may ask for a new license or an amendment to a previously negotiated license. If so, it is good practice to verify that the original fully executed license, with signatures by licensor and licensee, is on file. When it is not available, ask for a copy of the license. Agreements may vary, but most define the details of the purchase, such

45

as subscription period, cancellation clauses, perpetual access, authorized users, authentication method, fair use, permissions for interlibrary, and so on. More details on negotiating licenses are discussed in chapter 4.

Electronic resources are typically purchased directly with publishers or indirectly via resellers, consortia, agents, and jobbers. Each category of vendor has its own strengths and weaknesses. Publishers lacking retail expertise, such as associations and societies, may work with a reseller to distribute and market their publications. Ordering directly from the publisher or reseller can potentially reduce subscription costs and simplify reporting troubleshooting and access issues. When libraries purchase e-resources through consortia, they can achieve numerous benefits from collaborative collection development. Some of the most notable advantages include community building, member advocacy, license negotiations for new acquisitions and renewals, increased buying power, and greater access to shared collections. Some negative attributes of consortial activities include management issues such as time-consuming negotiations and coordination that lead to delays, inefficiencies, and ineffectiveness (Pan, 2010).

Publishers, resellers, and consortia generally do not offer acquisitions support services that are available from agents and jobbers. For example, these vendors negotiate with publishers on behalf of libraries and allow their customers to order items online, update ILMS order records automatically with EDIFACT (Electronic Data Interchange for Administration, Commerce, and Transport), and process invoices with EDI (Electronic Data Interchange). Manual record maintenance is very labor intensive and time-consuming. Although these services can be extremely helpful when staffing is limited, the agents and jobber charge additional fees for their assistance. In addition, ordering indirectly—through a reseller, consortium, agent, or jobber—adds another communication layer and creates more complexity to process. When choosing among different types of vendors, the librarian should weigh the pros and cons of financial discounts versus increased labor cost.

FACILITATING ACCESS AND DISCOVERY

Although chapter 5 discusses the following concepts and additional concepts in more detail, it is important to think about access and discovery in the context of the acquisition cycle. Librarians will want to ensure that the resource they are considering for purchase can be displayed in an acceptable manner for their institutional or organizational needs.

Identifying the vendor can also offer insight into the online location of the hosted content. During the acquisition phase, the librarian will want to know if the e-resource is provided on a familiar or unknown website or device, if an authentication method has been defined, and if the number of users is limited. In addition, the librarian should decide how and where the online content should be cataloged in the short and long term. The initial access and discovery setup process can begin once these answers are determined and vendor information is retained or distributed to appropriate colleagues.

For new web-based access, a resource may require activation or registration with the content provider. Shortly after an order has been submitted, the vendor typically e-mails the librarian contact details for technical service support and instructions with separate website addresses for the paid content and the librarian "portal." From this interface, the librarian may be able to obtain usage statistics, customize the resource for local needs, register access, update authentication information, or download bibliographic records.

The portal information will need to be managed by the librarian or passed along to responsible personnel. It is good practice to save the e-mail in a personal folder and also record the information so that it is available to others in an ERMS, ILMS, or a shared Word or Excel file. While troubleshooting an access problem, for instance, the librarian will need to find the technical support contacts as quickly as possible. Similarly, collection development librarians will want to consult usage statistics before making renewal decisions. It may be possible to customize the appearance or functionality of the electronic resources by uploading logos, modifying "welcome messages," or changing the results display order from publication date to relevancy.

To ensure that only authorized users are able to access the content, the publisher will need to verify or authenticate patrons for on and off campus. Standard authentication methods are username and password, IP address, and URL rewrite or proxy server (Conger, 2004). Regardless of the selected method, the setup during the acquisitions phase requires action by both the content provider and library staff and details are often recorded in the license agreement. The vendor usually creates the initial username and password, which sometimes can be changed later by library personnel. In turn, the library will need to find a method of managing and communicating the authentication information to the patron. To setup IP authentication, the content provider requests validation details from the library. With this configuration, on-campus patrons seamlessly access the electronic resource. The library will establish off-campus access by entering the content URL into the proxy server and displaying the modified URL on library webpages.

Libraries ideally have unlimited access to the e-resource. High prices may make unrestricted access cost prohibitive. Thus, a library might opt to provide for a few authorized users instead of denying everyone the opportunity to use the electronic resource. If there are any limitations, this information should be shared with the patron at the initial access point, such as a database A–Z list or the bibliographic record MARC field 856 (see figures 3.2 and 3.3).

Once the content has been made available, how will it be accessed by the patron? The librarian should determine the best method of making resources accessible and identifiable within library budgets and staffing limitations. Traditionally, the library catalog has been the primary gateway to library resources. More recently, libraries have been purchasing resource discovery services or software that enable patrons to search and retrieve content in all formats across multiple interfaces, such as library catalogs, article databases, and institutional repositories. Regardless of the selected solution, there are system costs and labor expenses to purchase and maintain the hardware, software, and/or service.

The librarian should consider the feasibility of cataloging resources on a collection or item level. For example, when purchasing an e-book collection, is the content cataloged on a database or title level? For small collections, it is possible to produce item-level MARC records in-house. Larger sets, however, require assistance from publishers offering free MARC records or vendors providing outsourced record services, or through purchasing WorldCat Collection Sets (OCLC, 2011). Either a cataloger or the librarian could be responsible for managing these activities. Beyond local MARC record catalogs, resource discovery also occurs between databases and by other libraries. Does the library subscribe to open URL resolver services to connect patrons to full-text content from abstract and index databases? Does the publisher allow interlibrary loan of electronic content, and does the library

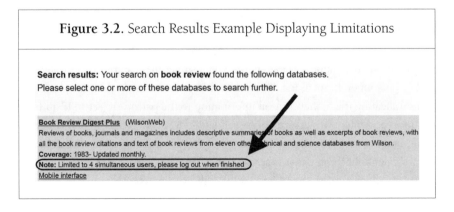

Figure 3.2. Search Results Example Displaying Limitations

Search results: Your search on **book review** found the following databases. Please select one or more of these databases to search further.

Book Review Digest Plus (WilsonWeb)
Reviews of books, journals and magazines includes descriptive summaries of books as well as excerpts of book reviews, with all the book review citations and text of book reviews from eleven other technical and science databases from Wilson.
Coverage: 1983- Updated monthly.
Note: Limited to 4 simultaneous users, please log out when finished
Mobile interface

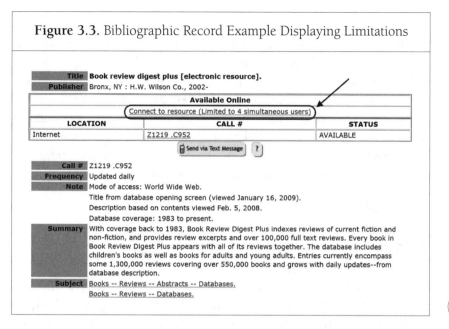

Figure 3.3. Bibliographic Record Example Displaying Limitations

have the means to share their holdings? If so, the librarian and/or colleagues will be tracking databases with Open URL resolver and updating holdings with OCLC to allow for resource sharing.

An additional complication is that downloading e-book content into a physical e-reader can create unforeseen implications for established work flows. There are potential disconnects between bibliographic records for the device and the electronic content. If acquisitions and cataloging roles are separated from the librarian, it is critical that the purchaser communicates the e-book titles for discovery in the catalog and access on a separate device that can be checked out. Traditional ILMSs are not designed to accommodate this relationship. As such, libraries have developed various workarounds to meet their needs.

For example, Winthrop University assigned each device a descriptive name and number, such as "Kindle 1" in the title field (MARC field 245) and call number field (MARC field 099), and the call number was shared with all of the e-book titles loaded on the device. Antje Mays (2010) explains that "because each title was given the same call number as the device on which it was loaded, the indexed call-number field leads library patrons to knowing which titles are loaded on which device" (p. 58). Mays (2010) warns that "the technological underpinnings have farther-reaching implications: not only do Acquisitions and Cataloging share the work; Library Systems, eBook suppliers, and ILS vendors also factor into eBook work flows—changes can be broad-based and reach beyond the Library" (p. 56).

When budgets are unpredictable, the librarian should also consider cancellation possibilities. Did the license agreement include termination clauses or stipulate perpetual access? As the licensee, the library may be required to give advance notice to end the subscription. To provide ongoing use of the content on the original platform the publisher may charge a hosting or access fee. For some one-time purchases, the vendor distributes electronic files of the purchased materials on a storage device or as a downloadable file. The library would be responsible for storing, preserving, and maintaining authenticated access to the data from their own institutional repository or via an outsource service, such as CLOCKSS (2011) or Portico (2011).

SUMMARY

Traditionally, the acquisition phase focused primarily on ordering, receiving, and paying for proprietary published materials. In the online environment, however, the responsibilities have expanded. When ordering electronic materials, librarians encounter more exceptions to the rule and cannot assume that the resource type will dictate work flow. Instead, other important traits should be considered—such as quantity, purchase type, costs, archival rights, vendor, and license terms—that will influence initial and ongoing purchase procedures. In addition, the librarian is responsible for gathering and distributing information that will determine the access and discovery setup process. The action items may be performed by the librarian or passed to other colleagues, depending on roles and responsibilities. Electronic resources are constantly changing and evolving. As such, this chapter is only an overview of considerations identified at one snapshot of time. By no means is it intended to be a definitive and exhaustive "encyclopedia" of acquisitions issues, but rather a sampling of possibilities in the online environment.

REFERENCES

CLOCKSS. 2011. "CLOCKSS: A Trusted Community-Governed Archive." CLOCKSS. February 24. www.clockss.org/clockss/.

Conger, Joan E. 2004. *Collaborative Electronic Resource Management*. Westport, CT: Libraries Unlimited.

Delquie, Emilie, and Cory Tucker. 2011. "Moving Forward with Electronic Content Procurement." *Against the Grain* 23, no. 5 (November): 22–28.

DeLuca, Carolyn, and Dani Roach. 2010. "Managing E-books: It Sounds Serial." Paper presented at Electronic Resources & Libraries, Austin, Texas, February.

Henderson, Kittie S., and Stephen Bosch. 2010. "Seeking the New Normal." *Library Journal* 135, no. 7 (April 15): 36–40. Library, Information Science & Technology Abstracts, EBSCOhost.

IRS (Internal Revenue Service). 2011a. "Request for Taxpayer Identification Number and Certification." Internal Revenue Service. January. www.irs.gov/instructions/iw9/.

———. 2011b. "Section 501(c)(3) Organizations." Internal Revenue Service. www.irs .gov/publications/p557/ch03.html.

Kerr, Sharon Hybki. 2010. "Electronic Resource Management Systems: The Promise and Disappointment. A Report of the Program Presented by the ALCTS Continuing Resources Section, Acquisitions Committee, American Library Association Annual Conference, Chicago, July 2009." *Technical Services Quarterly* 27, no. 3 (July): 297–300. Library, Information Science & Technology Abstracts with Full Text, EBSCOhost.

Mays, Antje. 2010. "Biz Acq Workflows in Paradise: eBooks, Acquisitions, and Cataloging." *Against the Grain* 22, no. 4 (September): 56–59. Library, Information Science & Technology Abstracts, EBSCOhost.

Miller, William. 2011. "Patron-Driven Acquisitions (PDA): The New Wave in Book Acquisitions Is Coming." *Library Issues* 31, no. 5 (May): 1–4. Library, Information Science & Technology Abstracts with Full Text, EBSCOhost.

OCLC. 2011. "WorldCat Collection Sets™." OCLC. www.oclc.org/worldcatsets/.

Pan, Denise. 2010. "Return on Investment for Collaborative Collection Development: A Cost-Benefit Evaluation of Consortia Purchasing." *Collaborative Librarianship* 2, no. 4: 183–192.

Portico. 2011. "Portico Services, Value and Benefits." Portico. www.portico.org/digital -preservation/services/.

Stemper, Jim, and Susan Barribeau. 2006. "Perpetual Access to Electronic Journals: A Survey of One Academic Research Library's Licenses." *Library Resources & Technical Services* 50, no. 2 (April): 91–109. Library, Information Science & Technology Abstracts, EBSCOhost.

Su, Di. 2007. "Introduction." *The Acquisitions Librarian* 19, no. 1/2: 1–2.

Tijerina, Bonnie. 2008. "Editorial." *Journal of Electronic Resources Librarianship* 20, no. 1: 1–2.

Chapter Four

Licensing Electronic Resources and Contract Negotiation

Ryan O. Weir

Although licensing may be one of the least favorite job duties of many librarians who manage an electronic resources collection, it is arguably the single most important one. This is because contract law, not copyright law, dictates how a resource may be used. If a librarian does not negotiate for the widest range of acceptable uses, the resource will not be as valuable to patrons as it could have been. All the information governing the access of a particular resource can be found in the license. Therefore, it is essential that the electronic resources librarian review licenses and, when possible, negotiate for terms that favor the library and its patrons.

Most librarians or other library professionals do not have a background in legal studies. This fact also adds to the complexity of being able to effectively manage an electronic resources collection. The legal world is filled with jargon, clauses, exemptions, guarantees, indemnities, responsibilities, and myriad other variables. It is a world that can be confusing, as well as overwhelming, for the layperson who is trying to interpret its complexities. This chapter provides strategies for managing work flows surrounding licensing, discusses the nature of a license (contract law) versus copyright law and negotiating contract terms, and in general seeks to give the reader a better understanding of licensing. The chapter examines licensing from both practical and historical viewpoints in the hope of providing readers with foundation knowledge that will better equip them to converse with vendors and organizational legal departments, and to negotiate the best license for their institutions. For an extra layer of complexity, electronic resources librarians at many publicly funded institutions must also follow state procurement rules. Once the license has been signed, the terms need to be translated from the legal jargon of the license into a simplified set of information so they can be communicated to library colleagues and patrons. This chapter offers some strategies on how to negotiate, organize, manage, and maintain licenses with or without an electronic resource management system (ERMS).

THE NATURE OF LICENSING AND CONTRACT LAW (LICENSING)

Understandably, the topic of licensing electronic resources through contract law has been covered extensively since the inception of electronic resources and licensing in the library world. Knowing the history of copyright and the relationships between and explanations of copyright law and contract law is essential when trying to explain these two radically different, and often misunderstood, topics to library stakeholders and patrons. "Licensing terms and copyright determine how clients and libraries use information resources" (Albitz, 2008: xix). This assertion defines the debate in its simplest terms. An electronic resources librarian must ensure that the library's patrons have as much freedom as possible to use the resources. It is important to remember the simple fact that when a license is signed, that license, not copyright law or fair use, governs what can and cannot be done with the purchased content. Only if flexibility is built into the language of the license will the end user have the desired flexibility in the use of the content. "To subscribe to most electronic journals and other electronic resources, you or someone at your institution will be required to sign a license. This is a legally binding contract, often written in legalese, potentially with many terms and provisions" (Curtis, 2004: 157). Again, librarians need to be aware that contract law trumps fair use and that by signing a license agreement the library states it understands that the terms within the contract, not copyright law, govern the use of the provided electronic resources. This concept will be repeated throughout this chapter, as it is one of the most, if not the most, important and often misunderstood concepts when dealing with licensing resources.

> "To subscribe to most electronic journals and other electronic resources, you or someone at your institution will be required to sign a license. This is a legally binding contract, often written in legalese, potentially with many terms and provisions."
> (Curtis, 2004: 157)

One set of clauses of concern to libraries within licensing agreements, among many others, is the interlibrary loan (ILL) use clauses. Since the inception of electronic journal content, the ability of libraries to continue to provide these materials via interlibrary loan as they have done in the past with print materials is, in many cases, still in question. Many publishers and vendors are becoming more willing to include these clauses, with some restrictions, in their agreements. Many others have made them standard to their generic license agreements. However, more progress is needed in this area of licensing.

Copyright versus Licensing

Many of the treatises on this topic have gone into great detail about the differences between contract law and copyright law—which actually supersedes the other and which should supersede the other. A simple approach to this topic is best. When signing a contract, assume that you are signing away all copyright exceptions *including* fair use, unless they are expressly stated in the contract that is signed on behalf of the institution or organization. So make sure to negotiate as many of these clauses directly into the language of the license and ensure that everything you want in the way of access and flexibility of use for a specific resource is spelled out in the final license document.

History of Copyright Leading into Contract Law

Until the introduction of electronic resources into libraries, the holdings of libraries and what libraries did with them were governed by copyright law and fair use provisions within that law. In the United States, the founding fathers understood the need for intellectual property to have limited protections in order to encourage thinkers, philosophers, and writers to engage in their crafts and thus perpetuate the evolution of our society through the shared knowledge and ideas of the persons making up that society. They understood that providing these protections would allow these writers to turn their ideas into profit for themselves and thus provide incentive for more creative thought and the sharing of those ideas to take place. Thus, copyright protections made their way into one

> "The Congress shall have power . . . to promote the progress of science and useful arts, by securing for limited times to authors and inventors the exclusive right to their respective writings and discoveries." (U.S. Constitution)

55

of the earliest documents created by the fledgling democratic republic, the Constitution of the United States.

Congress has continued to provide more protections for intellectual property throughout the years. The next major revision and expansion of copyright law occurred in 1976 with the addition of Title 17. Title 17 took copyright law a step further. Not only did Title 17 protect written information, it now encompassed other realms of intellectual and artistic creation including radio, TV, and film. Appendix A includes excerpts from many of the copyright documents that have been implemented historically in the United States.

LICENSES AND LICENSING AGREEMENTS

There are many types of license agreements. It is important for the librarian who works with contracts to be familiar with all types, as everything from the CD-ROM in the back of a science book to the aggregated databases that are prevalent in all types of libraries come with a set of restrictions either executed via signatures or assumed consent upon opening the item. There are two main types of licenses—an end user agreement and a site license agreement; both of these agreements, for the purposes of this chapter, would be made between a content or service provider and a library.

End User Agreement

This type of license agreement is usually click-through, shrink-wrap, or executable upon receipt of item—an agreement that stipulates the terms of use between the end user (patrons) and the vendor or publisher. These types of agreements are generally included in all types of consumer information products and services, including e-mail providers, blogs, iTunes, compact discs in the back of textbooks and other print media, and a variety of other types of products and services.

Site License Agreement (Negotiable License Agreement)

This type of agreement is generally used in libraries to license databases, journals, and other continuing electronic resources. It is an agreement that allows a library's patrons (single site or multisite) to use a given resource. It stipulates the provisions and requirements of both the licensee and licensor in respect to the use of the information and services provided. Sometimes these types of licenses may have limitations due to the amount a library is able to pay for the resources. These limitations may include but are not limited to the number of user seats allocated, or while becoming less common, the confinement of access to a one or more computer stations with dedicated IP (Internet protocol) addresses.

More and more libraries around the country are not only subscribing to access to content, but are purchasing the content outright. In many of these instances there are small continuation fees for the maintenance and upkeep of these products. In most cases these items are still licensed in order to spell out the responsibilities and rights of the provider and the library.

PARTS OF A TYPICAL LICENSE

Many licenses will include clauses stipulating that the license terms themselves are considered confidential. When the librarian comes across one of these clauses, he or she should seek to have it removed, or at the very least seek to limit the clause to ensure the clause is in compliance with state law and statutes. That being said, none of the following agreement section examples have been taken verbatim from license agreements currently or previously entered into by any organization.

License Introduction

This portion of the license generally stipulates who the licensee (e.g., the library) and the licensor (e.g., the vendor) of the agreement are, or in simple terms stipulates the two parties who are entering into the agreement. The term and start date of the license may be included in this section as well or may be stipulated elsewhere in the license. Many licenses

POSSIBLE ITEMS CONTAINED IN A LICENSE AGREEMENT

- Contact information
- Subscription periods
- IP address information
- Title lists
- Holding dates
- Prices
- Renewal dates
- Interlibrary loan/reserves usage
- Multi/single site
- Off-campus access
- Other unique clauses

stipulate this information in the payment and access schedule usually attached as an appendix to the document and contain a statement in the introduction referring to this section of the agreement.

For example, this section may read:

> This agreement (license) sets forth the terms and conditions under which (vendor name/address) and (school name/address) enter into an agreement for the access and use of the stipulated electronic resource(s) referenced in appendix I section 1.2 of this document.

Key Definitions

The key definitions section of the agreement generally defines all terms that will be used in the agreement. These terms may include but are not limited to the following:

- Product subject to license
- Licensee
- Licensor
- Authorized user (may or may not include a provision for "walk-ins")
- Single site
- Multisite
- User population (and how the size of that population is determined)

Access

This section defines the access to the content that the authorized users may or may not have. This section may also include clauses dealing with IP authentication, use of a proxy server, Athens authentication, and more. The variety of locations or access methods may affect the pricing of materials. It is important to note that pricing models and definitions of autho-

COMMON ELECTRONIC RESOURCE ACCESS TOOLS IN LIBRARIES

- Online public access catalogs (OPACs)
- E-resource portals such as A–Z lists
- Subject indexes
- Federated search engines
- Link resolvers
- Discovery layers
- Browsing lists such as database lists

rized sites and users may vary greatly from one content provider to the next. More information about access can be found in chapter 5.

Acceptable Use (Terms and Conditions of Use)

This section spells out what licensees may do with the content they have purchased. It may include provisions detailing download, storage of content, print rights, transmittal of e-content to other users outside/inside the individuals designated as authorized users, and inclusion in a library's OPAC.

This section is also where ILL and e-reserve rights may be stipulated. Many libraries in the past have made the assumption that if these rights are not explicitly forbidden, then it is okay to provide materials to other libraries via ILL and to place items on e-reserve. However, in reality, this is not the case. If these clauses are not in the agreement, *ask for them*. It is important for the librarian who is negotiating to know what the organization feels are deal breakers within a contract.

Prohibited Use or Definitions of Misuse and the Consequences for Misuse

This section is the counterpart to the section above and generally explicitly states what the user *cannot* do with the content and the penalties for this misuse. This may include whether a proxy server may be used, whether information can be accessed off campus, or any other restrictions. In many cases vendors do monitor their content for breaches of this section of the contract. For example, the vendor might notice an excessive amount of material being downloaded to a single IP address, which in most licenses violates acceptable use terms. If there is a breach, your institution will be contacted and asked to remedy the issue or be told that service will not be continued.

Licensee Responsibilities

As the heading implies, this section lays out the responsibilities of the licensee to the licensor. The library is the licensee. This section will most likely include language that states what restrictions and protections you must impose on content provision and users to ensure the content is used only by authorized users and in a manner consistent with the license terms and conditions.

Licensor Responsibilities

This section spells out the responsibilities of the licensor (the content provider) to the library. Generally this section will state that the content provider will ensure reliable access to the resource for a certain percentage of the time and will continue that access unless there is breach of terms of the contract or a situation out of their control limits access. Generally, reliability should be at or above 90–95 percent of the time; if the licensor fails to meet the stated reliability, ask for a discount or partial refund.

Term and Termination

This section specifies the term, or time period, of the contract and stipulates if the contract can be terminated, who can terminate the contract, and the reasons for which a contract can be terminated or renegotiated.

Other Provisions

This section or sections of the license may include any or all of the following:

- Confidentiality clauses—what can and cannot be disclosed about the license
- Jurisdiction—the location of the court in which legal disputes would be settled
- Indemnity clauses—variable clauses meant to indicate blamelessness
- Usage statistics—spells out what type of statistics the vendor will provide
- Back files—noncurrent content that may be allocated for free or for a fee
- Transactional access—the purchase of unsubscribed content on an article or chapter basis
- Package access—access to journal not subscribed to but on the publisher/vendor platform

Multiyear Provisions

Many times licenses may contain a multiyear provision, with terms that include the following:

- Price increase caps
- Cancellations from year to year
- Early termination
- Title switch out
- Minimum purchase amount

Generally, if a library agrees to sign a contract for multiple years, the contracted price per year should be lower than what would be offered for a single year, or at minimum there should be an agreement that when renewing the contract, there will be a guaranteed maximum percentage increase.

Signature Section for Authorized Signatories

At many libraries, this is the director of libraries, provost, president of the university, chairperson of the board, comptroller, or other designated entity either within the library itself or within the greater university or organization.

61

DEVELOPING A MODEL LICENSE OR LICENSE CHECKLIST

Developing a model license or license checklist is a fairly simple process. The first step of the process is to identify the terms and conditions that the organization desires to have included in all agreements. The librarian will need to consult the institution's legal department to ensure that all of the state and institutionally mandated terms are included. In addition, the librarian will need to consult a wide range of information sources in order to compile a complete list of terms and conditions to include in all license documents (see the example license documents sidebar as a start).

Once the institutional-specific list is compiled, each of the clauses needs to be categorized. The following is suggested terminology for the categories: required or negotiable. If the librarian would like to include more categories he or she may do so, but required and negotiable are the only two that need to be included. Now that a list of desired terms has been compiled and categorized, it is time to create either a model license or a license checklist. The checklist (see the sample provided) contains some of the items that may be found in a desired terms listing. A checklist is a simple, straightforward option, and also the one that is the easiest

EXAMPLE LICENSE DOCUMENTS

California Digital Library

- www.cdlib.org/gateways/vendors/docs/Model_License_LATEST_Revised_10 -08a.rtf

- www.cdlib.org/gateways/vendors/checklist.html

Yale Model License

- www.library.yale.edu/~llicense/standlicagree.1st.html

ALA Library and Licensing

- www.ala.org/ala/issuesadvocacy/copyright/librariesandlicensing/LibrariesAnd Licensing.cfm

to use when looking over and evaluating licenses. This option is recommended for those professionals just starting out with the process and will allow ease of evaluation and negotiation.

Remember to include as many items as needed to meet the legal requirements of the university or organization. Tailor the checklist to the individualized institutional needs. It is also important to approach negotiations with a goal of coming to a mutually beneficial agreement in which both parties receive what they need from the other.

CONTRACT NEGOTIATION

In order to be successful in license negotiation, keep in mind that, as in any successful conversation, a contract negotiation must be a two-way street. Do not get entirely caught up in the library's issues. The negotiation process can differ greatly from vendor to vendor and from year to year with the same vendor if there is a change in sales representative, which tends to happen quite often. See the contract negotiations sidebar for some things to keep in mind when starting on the process of negotiating and going through the approval process of licensing.

CONTRACT NEGOTIATION CHECKLIST

Date: _____

Vendor/Publisher: _____

Product: _____

Required Terms

❑ The contract is to be governed by the laws of the United States and the Commonwealth of Kentucky.

❑ Strike any confidentiality clauses or add "Subscriber agrees, to the extent allowed by the laws of the Commonwealth of Kentucky."

❑ Strike indemnity clauses or add "Subscriber agrees, to the extent allowed by the laws of the Commonwealth of Kentucky."

❑ ILL use is explicitly mentioned in the agreement.

❑ Financial hardship clause is included (*be specific here*): Defined as a 20 percent reduction in the library's continuations budget.

Negotiable Terms

❑ Electronic reserve explicitly mentioned in the agreement.

❑ Perpetual access provisions are included.

❑ Pay-per-view discount for materials not subscribed.

❑ Price increase cap per year on multiyear agreements.

❑ Percentage cancellation per year of multiyear agreements.

❑ Refund for early termination due to financial hardship.

❑ Counter/SUSHI-compliant usage statistics.

❑ Back-file access.

❑ Other: _____

POINTS TO REMEMBER ABOUT CONTACT NEGOTIATIONS

- Everything generally takes more time than anticipated.

- Most vendors will be willing to turn on trial or full access during this process if asked. They may not always offer.

- Vendors can always do better than their first offer.

- Unable to get the terms you desire from sales representatives? Ask them to take the requests to their supervisor. Usually the supervisor can do more than the salesperson can do alone.

- Foster positive relationships with salespeople. They will be more likely to work harder on your behalf.

- Don't be afraid to offer multiyear options or additional purchases; just make sure you get your money's worth if you do.

- Negotiating can be an enjoyable and engaging experience if you are organized and you know your limitations.

The following steps will get the negotiations off to a good start:

- Establish rapport with the person on the other side of the negotiations. Make sure to communicate preferred contact methods for yourself and the representative. Find out if the vendor will be able to approve all changes or if the sales representative will need to get approval during the process for certain changes. Emphasize that you understand that the negotiation needs to be mutually beneficial.

- Know the contract and make sure to review it. It is acceptable to ask questions to clarify portions of the contract if the wording is unclear or if something is not included in the language.

- Know the license requirements of the institution, both pie in the sky and practical. Make sure to identify any present or missing contract terms that could be a deal breaker for the institution. Communicate these needs first and then proceed to the other portions of the negotiation. Make sure to explain why something is a deal breaker and explain preferred or acceptable options.

- Ask for what you want. The only sure way not to achieve a beneficial agreement is not to ask for desired provisions. In addition to priority requests, be sure to make the deal breakers known. Don't be afraid to push for better terms in any agreement. Also keep in mind that if the sales representative can only go so far, usually a supervisor has more leeway to negotiate better terms. For example, if a sales rep for a vendor can only negotiate a 10 percent discount, a supervisor may be able to go to 30 percent; don't be afraid to ask to speak with a supervisor. A librarian may be able to negotiate for better rates by offering to buy more volume or committing to more than one year for an agreement term.

INSTITUTIONAL/ORGANIZATIONAL APPROVAL PROCESS

The most important things to keep in mind when dealing with any set of information are organization of the information and organization of the work flow behind the information and its use. When licensing electronic resources, this also holds true. The librarian tasked with working with electronic resources will deal with a very large number of licensing agreements during a given year. Some of these agreements may be simple renewals of agreements that have been settled on in the past, while others may be entirely new contracts that will need extensive review. In some cases, licensing language is placed at the bottom of invoicing, with clauses stating that the language contained will go into effect upon payment of the invoice. There will also be less conventional agreements such as click-through agreements, shrink-wrap agreements, passive-assent agreements, and various other types of agreements that are thrown at both libraries and individual citizens on a daily basis.

Know the process of the university or organization for which the resource is being purchased. The processes and methods used within libraries to evaluate and approve invoices vary greatly. The variations run the gamut, from an electronic resources librarian agreeing to license agreements without the consultation or approval of any higher authority within the institutional hierarchy, to every agreement, no matter how small, having to go through a legal department, the director, chairman of the board, dean, provost, or president before approval can be granted. One would think that this many steps would be a cumbersome process that would be very slow and inefficient, but in many cases even when other departments such as purchasing, accounting, or information technology get involved, the licensing contract can normally be turned around in less than two weeks. This system is beneficial because it ensures multiple points of review and no one person is responsible for the approval of the license, although in reality, if there were an issue, the ultimate responsibility would lie with the library professional who is purchasing the material. While the signatory has the ultimate legal responsibility, he or she will be coming back to the professional who purchased the content and reviewed the license if there are issues arising from the agreement. It is important for all involved to be comfortable with the system and the process that is in place at the institution.

Once a system has been established for approving contracts, it is important to become familiar with the people in that system and establish a rapport with them. It is important for the signatories and other reviewers to know who the library representative is when a cover letter with their name on it comes across their

65

desk. Develop a process based on the larger university or institutional process. As an example, a librarian or other professional could use the following procedure:

- Print all agreements and review them for the changes; flag potential issues as well. Then create a cover letter to the legal department stating the name of the resource and request that the attached agreement be reviewed for conflicts with state law or university policy.
- Forward the document to the vendor or publisher with a list of requests for negotiation. License negotiations will be discussed in the next section of this chapter.
- Forward a hard copy of the agreement with a cover letter to the individual who actually signs the agreement. It is important to put a placeholder in the in-process folder with basic information about the agreement to ensure you do not lose track of the agreement status. It is also important to keep in mind that the process of licensing may take longer than initially anticipated, depending on the number and scope of the changes that need to be negotiated.
- Once the agreement is signed, a copy is returned to the publisher.
- When the countersigned copy is received from the publisher or vendor, the agreement can simply be scanned and sent to the publisher via e-mail. The organization should retain a hard copy and a digital copy of all license agreements.

SERU: ONE OPTION FOR USING RESOURCES WITHOUT A LICENSE

SERU, or Shared Electronic Resource Understanding, is a collaborative endeavor of NISO (National Information Standards Organization) and a variety of publishers and vendors to bypass the need for and process of licensing electronic resources. It is a viable option for libraries to use if a provider has signed on to the initiative. It serves as a statement of

SERU RESOURCES

- The SERU agreement can be found at www.niso.org/publica tions/rp/RP-7-2008.pdf.

- A listing of the libraries and information providers that subscribe to the SERU initiative is available at www.niso.org/ workrooms/seru/registry/.

- Organizations can sign on to SERU at www.niso.org/work rooms/seru/registry/signup/.

mutual understanding and of basic responsibilities of information providers and libraries in respect to purchased electronic resource content. This agreement serves as a way to save time and money expended during the licensing of e-resources.

SUMMARY

Ask for the stars; settle on a mutually beneficial agreement founded in trust and honesty! Know what the institution requires in contract negotiation before entering negotiation. Also, know the other negotiating partner and the likely needs and desires of the end users. Being prepared for a negotiation is paramount for the success of the negotiation. Licensing review and negotiation cannot be taken lightly, but it can be easily managed.

REFERENCES

Albitz, Becky. 2008. *Licensing and Managing Electronic Resources.* 1st ed. London: Chandos Publishing.

Curtis, Donnelyn. 2004. *E-Journals: A How-To-Do-It Manual for Building, Managing, and Supporting Electronic Journal Collections.* New York: Neal Shuman.

"The United States Constitution." www.house.gov/house/Constitution/Constitution.html.

Chapter Five

Making Electronic Resources Accessible

George Stachokas

Providing access to electronic resources is a crucial function of the modern library—academic, public, special, or school. This chapter reviews authentication, eight different types of online access tools, vendor administrative modules (VAMs), troubleshooting and technology support, and the ongoing maintenance and development of all of these tools as part of an overall access system for electronic resources (ASER). This chapter also addresses the need to consider user experience when providing access to electronic resources. Given rapid changes in technology and vendor-specific requirements, detailed instructions for setting up and maintaining specific tools are not provided, but general issues are addressed. Examples of specific vendors and products are included for clarity, but these references do not constitute any explicit or implied endorsement. Readers are strongly encouraged to investigate particular products and online access and discovery tools that meet their own needs.

Although an electronic resource management system (ERMs) is not an online access tool per se, it is, at the time of this writing, the single best tool for addressing problems of electronic resource management. There are a number of commercially available products, as well as some open-source tools. Some notable examples include Serials Solutions' 360 Resource Manager, Innovative Interfaces' Electronic Resource Management, EBSCONET's ERM Essentials, ExLibris's Verde, and CORAL, developed by the University of Notre Dame. The ASER is technically the front end, but without back-end support by an ERMS, the library will not be able to provide the many thousands of accurate URLs, coverage dates, license terms, and other metadata that must be continuously updated to provide information services for today's users. Acquiring and maintaining a good ERMS is strongly recommended.

AUTHENTICATION

Electronic resources, especially resources that require payment for access, can be used only if library patrons have the appropriate equipment, such as computers, e-readers, mobile devices, and so forth, and the library has taken the appropriate steps to provide access. Vendors and publishers protect their licensed content by requiring authentication by users. In the United States the most common authentication options are username and password–based access and IP (Internet protocol) authentication. While username and password access does work and is straightforward, it is impractical to implement at most libraries and remain in compliance with licensing terms requiring only authorized users' access. IP authentication is in most instances the preferred mode of providing authentication. When using IP authentication, a library provides a vendor or publisher with a list of IPs that contain the Internet protocol addresses of the institution or organization. If the library wishes to give patrons access outside that designated IP range, the patron may be assigned a log-in specific to the database, or implement the use of a proxy server. A proxy server allows patrons with log-in credentials to log in to the proxy server. This makes the patron's computer appear to be within the IP ranges of the organization or institution and thus the patron is allowed to gain access to the content as if at the library. After the authentication method is chosen and implemented, it is time to decide how the library will provide access to the resources.

ONLINE ACCESS TOOLS

Libraries provide access to electronic resources primarily through the following broad categories or types of online access tools:

- Online public access catalogs (OPACs)
- E-resource portals such as A–Z lists
- Subject indexes
- Federated search engines

- Link resolvers
- Discovery services
- Browsing lists such as database lists
- Embedded lists such as links in webpages in which the webpages are not specifically designed to deliver or provide access to electronic resources (e.g., a library guide about deforestation that includes a link to an environmental database)

These eight online access types or categories do not cover every imaginable delivery system for electronic resources, but they do serve as a useful conceptual model for considering how most patrons may access electronic resources in the modern library. Some libraries may be able to afford to acquire online access tools in each of these eight categories; other libraries may have to omit more recent innovations such as discovery layers. Local implementations of each category or type of online access tool will vary, but minimal standards for each of these systems must be taken into account in order to successfully deliver information to patrons.

Catalogs or OPACs

The online public access catalog (OPAC) is the public interface or front end of the integrated library system (ILS). The ILS usually consists of interrelated modules for staff use such as cataloging, acquisitions, and circulation modules. The OPAC has permitted generations of library patrons from the 1970s to search for content by author, title, alternate title, publisher, publication date, format, and many other characteristics depending on overall system capability and the underlying quality of cataloging. The first OPACs were developed before graphic user interfaces (GUIs) like Windows or Apple GS/OS, were quite rudimentary in appearance, and were entirely closed systems. Patrons searched within the catalog to locate materials owned within the library, and that was it. Now, most OPACs are complex webpages in their own right and require special consideration in terms of design and interoperability with other systems and tools, but for the electronic resources professional, the first consideration is cataloging, the creation and maintenance of resource records that describe the actual information resources that patrons are searching for in the first place. So, the first concern regarding the OPAC is MARC.

Machine-Readable Cataloging (MARC) was first developed in the 1960s by Henriette Avram of the Library of Congress (Rather and Wiggins, 1989), and while it predates the term "metadata," it arguably remains the single most extensively used form of metadata in twenty-first century libraries. Created for use on what is now outdated technology and lamented by some librarians for its limitations (Tennant, 2002), MARC records still far outnumber all other types of library resource records, with literally billions of records representing information resources in all formats all over the world. The record structure of MARC 21, the most recent version of MARC revised in 1996, is an implementation of ISO 2709 (ANSI/NISO Z39.2). The content that is stored in MARC records is entered as per the *Anglo-American Cataloguing Rules*, Second Edition, or AACR2. *Resource Description and Access* (RDA), a new cataloging standard, was developed in recent years as an attempt to improve upon the AACR2 rules to meet contemporary information needs (Miksa, 2009). RDA is more informed by what is called *Functional Requirements for Bibliographic Records* (FRBR), which is especially relevant for electronic resources and other new formats. Problems still remain, however, in that adaptations of cataloging rules for MARC still do not account for the level of granularity desired by most patrons, e.g., metadata at the article level (Wakimoto, 2009).

The ILS was developed around MARC. The primary resource record or bibliographic record created and maintained in the cataloging module typically is attached to financial records in the acquisitions module that are in turn associated with patron records as required by circulation status. Electronic resources librarians need not concern themselves with the circulation module or serials check-in, unless the librarian also has responsibility for print materials or other formats, but cataloging electronic resources is essential in order to be able to find and access databases, electronic journals, and e-books through the online catalog. Electronic resources—online resources—have posed many challenges for the ILS and OPAC from their inception. MARC records have had to be adapted for electronic resources, an ongoing process with mixed results. The single most important adaptation is the inclusion of an 856 field that includes a uniform resource locator (URL) or link to access an electronic resource directly. The link is usually displayed in the OPAC or online catalog when a record is discovered by a patron.

Descriptive fields, location codes, and other special fields were developed in MARC for physical materials, mostly printed books and serials. The MARC record was not designed with electronic resources in mind. The quality of MARC records for electronic resources has been poor partly due to the challenges of this new format, but also due to recent changes in libraries. Electronic resources emerged in force during the 1990s when many libraries began to increase automation and reduce staffing levels for routine work processes such as cataloging, and online access was perceived as somehow alien or separate from traditional library services.

Many catalogers did not know how to apply cataloging standards to electronic resources, and many proponents of electronic resources did not care about cataloging standards that they perceived as being overly rigid and outmoded. As electronic resources have shifted from the periphery to the center of the contemporary academic library, it is important to maintain MARC records of reasonably good quality for electronic resources, at least if the library still maintains an ILS and an OPAC.

To ensure that patrons find what they need, librarians should pay particular attention to correct titles (MARC 245 and 246 fields), ISSNs (MARC 022), ISBNs (MARC 020), publishers (MARC 260), and authors, if applicable (MARC 1XX or MARC 7XX for added entries), and ensure that the correct URLs are included in 856 fields. Being able to search by location codes and other fields may be less important, although the librarian still might want to know the total number of e-books held, for example. Including appropriate subject indexes in MARC records for electronic resources or 6XX fields is also very important, and some librarians include more than three subject fields for electronic resources.

It is highly recommended to create a template for different types of electronic resources records that indicate the minimum number of required MARC fields or tags, including any local customization, note fields, and other unique coding features required to ensure the maximum discoverability and access for patrons. These template(s) can then be shared with automation services or with other library personnel to ensure that standards are met. Responsibility and authority for cataloging electronic resources varies among libraries. Sometimes electronic resources librarians are entirely or partly responsible, but given low staffing levels, most professionals must typically undertake a process of negotiation and education with their colleagues to ensure that work is done correctly and promptly.

The OPAC itself, the actual user interface, is also important to consider for discoverability and access of electronic resources. Again, the individual librarian may have limited or no authority to change the underlying structure of the OPAC itself, and the appearance and design of an OPAC can vary quite a bit and still serve its fundamental purpose. What is most essential to consider is that electronic resources are clearly indicated as such in search results because a patron's search could pull multiple results in an equal number of different formats. Second, links must be functional and sufficiently prominent to be obvious to patrons at a single glance and not easily confused with other types of links that may appear on the OPAC results page such as widgets, help links, or other library links.

To summarize, the underlying technology and organization of the OPAC was designed before libraries acquired large numbers of electronic journals, databases, and e-books, but librarians must work to ensure that users can access electronic content in the most intuitive and convenient manner possible. At minimum, this process will require good MARC records with clearly visible working links. At best, any redesign or configuration of the OPAC should take the unique requirements of electronic resources into account, including, but not limited to, being able to limit and sort searches by format, show precise coverage dates for electronic journals, display user limits if applicable, and specify any special technology or authentication requirements.

E-resource Portals

E-resource portals are systems specifically developed to enable patrons to search for and access online content. The most obvious example is the A–Z list, a tool developed at the turn of the twenty-first century (Corbett, 2006). The first A–Z list was designed to enable patrons to search for journals by title or ISSN. Searches would then bring up a very brief resource record that included the appropriate hyperlink. The A–Z list allows patrons to find a specific electronic journal quickly. Library personnel are not required to perform the kind of complex cataloging work required with MARC records. Instead, library personnel simply select or track journals to which their institution subscribes from a much larger knowledge base or collection of resource records maintained by the vendor. Most electronic resources have more than one available link to access content in a typical knowledge base; however, it is often necessary to select the best possible link or multiple links. Library personnel must then make sure to keep track of multiple links/resource records for a single electronic resource, making any necessary changes as subscription status and access terms change over time. It is still necessary to test and troubleshoot access, but the process is considerably more streamlined and simplified, with much of the work being performed by vendors rather than library personnel (Mi, Sullenger, and Loghry, 2006).

Since most e-resource portals are provided by vendors and are not webpages developed by library personnel, it is important to consider the problem of branding. Marking an e-resource portal with the name of the institution or organization, library, and any appropriate consortia or other affiliations is essential for reminding patrons of who is paying for access but also lets patrons know that they are in the right place to find library electronic resources. Most commercially available systems include detailed instructions and resources for branding. Marking what the library pays for with appropriate and attractive text and imagery should not be considered as an afterthought, but as an integral part of service (Gall, 2010).

Since 2000, many vendors provide comparable products. Notable products include, but are not limited to, Serials Solutions' 360 Core, EBSCO A-to-Z, and Ex Libris's SFX. Some vendors also provide subject browsing for electronic journals, comparable functionality for e-books, database lists, and search functionality all integrated into a single webpage or portal. Providing access through an e-resource portal is simpler in some respects than providing access through an OPAC, but there are also additional considerations. Some e-resource portals also have the capability to display permitted uses and other relevant information contained in license agreements for electronic resources, but usually only if the library has implemented an ERMS that tracks this information. A–Z lists may provide the minimal necessary functionality, but even these tools increasingly require back-end support from a well-maintained ERMS to provide relevant information to contemporary users.

Subject Indexes

Subject indexes are searchable databases that index articles and other scholarly output in specific subject areas or academic disciplines. Some examples include AncestryPlus, Historical Abstracts for European History, Chilton's Automotive Repair, LISTA for library and information science, PubMED, and CINAHL for nursing and allied health. Some subject indexes provide only citations with abstracts. These resources are sometimes referred to as A&I databases or subject indexes at the Abstract & Index level. Other subject indexes include full text. Sometimes vendors offer both A&I versions and full-text versions of the same subject index, and perhaps most confusingly, multiple full-text versions with different levels of access to accommodate the purchase of these resources by a variety of library types. For example, at the time of writing, CINAHL is available from EBSCO in four different versions: CINAHL, CINAHL with Full Text, CINAHL Plus, and CINAHL Plus with Full Text. Testing and confirming the precise level of access for a subject index is important, but even more important is providing appropriate description and branding to reduce possible confusion among patrons.

Most libraries provide access to subject indexes through some kind of browsing list; some institutions go further and offer the capability to search for these resources by title or subject. Providing some kind of description ranging from a few sentences of text to a paragraph or two is highly beneficial to patrons, as this will help them to determine if a given resource is appropriate for their research needs.

Aggregators are large databases that include subject indexing for multiple disciplines and include full text coverage for many journals. Examples include EBSCO's Academic Search Premier, ProQuest Research Library, Gale's Expanded

Academic ASAP, and Informatic India's J-Gate (the paid version) and Open J-Gate (the free version). The largest aggregators include full-text coverage for thousands of titles, although it is not uncommon for the most recent six months or one year of coverage to be omitted. This exclusion of the most recently published content is commonly referred to as an embargo; embargos often range from a few months to a year in duration. Most aggregators provide content published in electronic journals, but some aggregators focus on e-books instead and an increasing number provide both electronic journal and e-book content. Many aggregators also provide indexing for titles not included with full text.

Federated Search Engines

Federated search engines permit patrons to search multiple subject indexes simultaneously. Notable products include Innovative Interfaces' Research Pro, Serials Solutions' 360 Search, Ex Libris's MetaLib, Google Scholar, and EBSCOhost Integrated Search. Vendors usually provide detailed setup instructions or provide direct assistance. Since there may be some important differences in how these resources are configured and this chapter is not intended to endorse specific products, this section will be necessarily short and mostly limited to a discussion of the appropriate role of federated search engines as a tool in the contemporary library.

Most federated search engines provide access to a limited number of subject indexes or databases, and most require annual subscription fees (Linoski and Walczyk, 2008). Adding additional databases to the federated search engine usually costs more money. Electronic resources professionals are encouraged to think carefully about what kind of subject indexes should be included; it may be wise to consult with other library personnel or refer the decision to some other authority within the library. If possible, it could be helpful to consult with patrons.

Federated search engines should be prominently placed on library webpages that include them and also clearly advertised as such (Ellis, Hartnett, and Waldman, 2008). Patrons should not be allowed to confuse federated search with specific subject indexes. Federated search is best thought of as a general search tool and may not be as useful for professional research. Undergraduates and those searching outside their field tend to benefit most from the use of federated search, but like any other tool, the value of federated search is dependent on sound design and implementation.

Link Resolvers

Link resolvers are essential for permitting patrons to check for the availability of full text when searching for articles in subject indexes. Link resolvers work or do not work to the degree that a given information resource is OpenURL compliant, otherwise known as NISO/ANSI standard Z39.88. To put it simply, OpenURL is a standard format of URL that enables users to find an appropriate copy of a given resource while searching a database or other discovery tool, more specifically in the case of libraries, an article or other full-text resource that users of a specific library are licensed to access. Link resolvers parse the elements of an OpenURL and then provide links to appropriate copies or targets that are available from the library's holdings. To work, OpenURL elements for electronic journals and e-books must be stored in an OpenURL knowledge base that includes relevant metadata including specific subscription terms and/or coverage dates. It is most convenient for libraries to customize or manage these knowledge bases through their ERMS, but some A–Z lists and other tools may provide the minimal necessary functionality. Maintaining these knowledge bases requires constant updating from publishers, aggregators, and other content providers, so the most crucial information in the supply chain cannot usually be provided by libraries. To promote the development and improvement of common standards, the United Kingdom Serials Group (UKSG) and the National Information Standards Organization (NISO) set up the Knowledge Bases and Related Tools (KBART) initiative in 2008. The transfer of titles between vendors is just one of many problems that must be addressed to ensure an accurate knowledge base (Hutchens, 2011).

LINK RESOLVER EXAMPLES
• EBSCO's LinkSource
• Innovative Interfaces' WebBridge
• Serials Solutions' 360 Link
• Ex Libris's SFX (also listed as an A–Z list)

Some examples include, but are not limited to, EBSCO's LinkSource, Innovative Interfaces' WebBridge, Serials Solutions' 360 Link, and Ex Libris's SFX (also listed as an A–Z list). Patrons can access link resolver results or check for availability by clicking on a small text message or icon typically located at the bottom of each citation on the search results page of a database or subject index. Link resolvers typically display as a separate webpage or pop-up window in which results are shown that indicate if the desired article or book chapter is available in the library's collection, along with a URL that directly leads to the desired resource. Designing link resolver pages that are simple and intuitive to use is necessary to get the best value from these tools. It is important to note that not all electronic resources are OpenURL compliant. This means that link resolvers will only work with part of the collection and some searches will still need to be conducted by other means. There are open access versions of link resolvers, but the most commonly used link resolvers are commercial products available from vendors by annual subscription.

Discovery Services

Discovery services, also referred to as discovery layers, are increasingly important for libraries. Some examples include Serials Solutions' AquaBrowser, Innovative Interfaces' Encore, SirsiDynix Enterprise, and EBSCO Discovery Service. Vendors are constantly working on improving this technology, providing more advanced web scale discovery services that far exceed the capabilities of earlier discovery layers; for example, Serials Solutions offers the more advanced Summon product in addition to AquaBrowser. All of these tools are touted as being a replacement for the traditional online catalog, or OPAC, as well as A–Z lists, other e-resource portals, and most other webpages used to find electronic resources. These flexible tools have been designed with Google in mind (Brubaker, Leach-Murray, and Parker, 2011) and enable patrons to start looking for resources using a simple search box. Searches can then be refined in multiple ways. Most discovery layers provide tags that appear in boxes or windows adjacent to search results that suggest other terms to search by. Multiple suggestions for refining results also appear with clickable links for publication data, geographical location, language, location, author, title, and other characteristics. The initial results can also usually be resorted by data, relevance, and so on, as with many other online searching tools. Discovery layers sometimes change search results based on the activities of users, such as bookmarking, printing, or saving content, past search history, and user-created lists.

Technology changes rapidly and has been improved considerably over time, but current constraints on the quality of data, competition among vendors, and the needs of

---

DISCOVERY SERVICES EXAMPLES

- Serials Solutions' AquaBrowser

- Innovative Interfaces' Encore

- SirsiDynix Enterprise

- Ex Libris's Primo

- EBSCO Discovery Service

- Summon

professional specialists reduce the overall value of discovery layers somewhat. Discovery layers still rely on resource records or metadata in order to provide access to content. Results in discovery layers are still only as good as the data that these results are based on. Metadata for discovery layers is provided by primary and secondary publishers (Vaughan, 2011b), but most aggregators and subject indexes refuse to share data with the developers of discovery layers due to perceived competition. Searching a well-supported discovery layer will produce valuable results for most patrons but may not provide the kind of focused in-depth results suitable for advanced research in highly specialized fields. Only the careful use of subject indexes can provide the latest and best research in biology, chemistry, physics, or psychology. Discovery layers can serve as a primary search tool for monographs and replace many functions formerly reserved for the traditional OPAC, often with greater ease of use and accuracy, but searching for articles is not yet as highly developed due to the problem of indexing.

More recently developed web scale discovery services such as Serials Solutions' Summon and other tools such as Ex Libris's Primo and EBSCO Discovery Service (EDS) provide vastly improved access to articles. Summon is based on a unified central index built from the ground up (Vaughan, 2011a), at least at the time of writing. While specific web scale discovery services may not truly index all available content (Wisniewski, 2010), the technology of web scale discovery services is a considerable improvement in comparison to the next generation catalog since it essentially provides a single search box for nearly all library resources (Breeding, 2010).

Marshall Breeding has noted how the new discovery layers can provide a single entry point for library users and enable users to search all types of content held within library collections (Breeding, 2009). As discovery layers improve, libraries may not need to invest in the currently diverse body of online access tools. Users tend to value convenience and the ability to search for information resources on their own. Investment in discovery layers, even more so web scale discovery services, is highly recommended for libraries. Some specialized users will still need to consider subject indexes and other tools, but a powerful, accurate, and convenient single search tool for libraries seems imperative as a gateway or front door to the online library.

Browsing Lists

Browsing lists are webpages, usually developed using only HTML and CSS, that include a list of links for electronic resources, typically subject indexes and other databases. Patrons simply browse through the list of links and click in order to access content. Browsing lists for databases, or database lists, vary somewhat in complexity and design and include multiple interrelated webpages, but what separates browsing lists from portals is the need to scroll through static webpages to find content. At a minimum, databases should be listed by some discernible order such as an alphabetical or subject list. URLs should be listed along with the commonly used title of the resource and the minimum amount of description necessary for the user to determine the value of using a particular resource for their research. Browsing lists work best for databases and some reference e-books, but should not be the primary method for accessing other types of electronic resources. Many libraries have either created their own webpages for this purpose or subscribed to a service such as LibGuides provided by SpringShare LCC (Becker, 2009), which offers a user-friendly web development option that allows users with minimal technical skills to create their own webpages.

Embedded Lists

Occasionally subject guides or other webpages created by library personnel for another purpose than providing access to electronic resources will also include links to electronic resources. Subject librarians or other professionals may create LibGuides or other webpages specifically tailored to an individual subject, class or content area and embed lists of library resources pertaining to those topics within the larger LibGuide. While these webpages have not been created with the purpose of providing access to electronic resources, some patrons may use these paths of access nonetheless. Embedded lists are very similar to browsing lists, with the distinction that the list of electronic resources is embedded or contained in a webpage designed for a different purpose than simply providing direct access to electronic resources. While electronic resources professionals may have limited or no control over these particular links, especially if these webpages are maintained by reference librarians or other personnel, patrons will expect links to commonly used electronic resources to work. This is a judgment call, and maintenance and access to more obscure or specialized resources should probably remain outside the responsibility of specialists in electronic resources.

VENDOR ADMINISTRATIVE MODULES

Many electronic resources provided by vendors include access to administrative websites, modules (known as vendor administrative modules, or VAMs), or other systems that electronic resources professionals can use to configure or customize electronic resources. One prominent example of a VAM is EBSCONET. Librarians should consider not only the eight major categories of online access tools but also how the functionality and access to databases and electronic journals are configured using these modules. Access to a VAM usually requires a unique username and password. Most libraries will have access to dozens of VAMs. Some of these administrative modules permit only minimal customization, but most permit some branding, for example, the inclusion of text and icons unique to the specific library to inform patrons that they are using resources paid for by the library. Most of these modules provide access to Counting Online Usage of Networked Electronic Resources (COUNTER)–compliant usage statistics. Even if a library has a Standardized Usage Statistics Harvesting Initiative (SUSHI) client and pulls usage statistics automatically, the unique username and password for the VAM are still required for use by the client to access usage data. VAMs can also enable library personnel to set up link resolvers, select different options for the display and functionality of databases, set up user groups, and, in some cases, even monitor usage by individuals. So, it is extremely important to keep track of VAMs, store log-in information in a safe place, be careful to share log-in information with authorized personnel only, and observe all applicable laws and institutional rules regarding privacy and the confidentiality of library data.

TROUBLESHOOTING AND TECHNOLOGY SUPPORT

Unlike print materials, electronic resources require troubleshooting and technical support. Broken links are a common problem due to technical problems experienced by vendors and platform changes or upgrades, as well as unresolved or unknown problems with payment processing. Most electronic resources also require routine maintenance, as content providers must upgrade their systems and maintain technology similar to other online content providers.

Maintenance alerts are usually announced by library vendors, often in e-mail or other electronic correspondence. Alerts can also be set up in many ERMSs. Electronic resources librarians should take the time to review these messages, taking careful note of the length of downtime and any other important information. Maintenance alerts should be shared with colleagues, including public service personnel such as reference/instruction librarians and staff. Posting alerts on library webpages is also advised, depending on the length of downtime and potential inconvenience to the user.

Some technical problems can be addressed by library personnel, but most require action by vendors. Most vendors have separate contacts for sales and technical support, but this is not always the case. It is important to report problems to vendors promptly and then to request as much additional information as possible. While waiting for a problem to be addressed by a vendor, electronic resources librarians should contact their colleagues and advise patrons to assure them that the problem is being addressed by the vendor. How much and when to advise about troubleshooting is a judgment call, but it is crucial for professionals to (1) acknowledge receipt of the problem and (2) advise that the problem will be addressed by library personnel and/or library vendors. Without criticizing the vendor too much, library personnel should avoid taking responsibility for problems that can be addressed only by the vendor; they can instead express sympathy for any inconvenience and keep patrons informed of progress on the resolution.

USER EXPERIENCE

Vendors and other commercial entities involved in information technology have embraced user experience (UX) in the design of their products for several decades. Wayne Bivens-Tatum has pointed out that the rich and complex UX literature covers a number of topics, ranging from information architecture to human-computer interaction, but the most essential lesson for librarians should be sympathy for the user. We need to design our webpages and search portals with the user's needs, convenience, and utility always in mind (Bivens-Tatum, 2010). Librarians also have to sell a product, our information services, and design our information delivery systems to encourage our users to avail themselves of our services.

Taking UX seriously requires us to look beyond questions of productivity, efficiency, and instrumentality in web design. Is the library's website attractive to users? Is it fun and easy to use? How is the specific clientele that uses a particular library actually going to use the library's online resources? Marc Hassenzahl and Noam Tractinsky have mapped out some of the complexity of UX, indicating that it is a consequence of a user's internal state (mood, personal motivation, predisposition, etc.), the characteristics of the designed system, and the context or environment in which the interaction occurs (Hassenzahl and Tractinsky, 2006).

Implementing an ASER that takes user experience into account requires getting to know one's users. Direct input from users is required when designing library webpages, configuring search and discovery tools provided by vendors, and considering how the library manages all of its services. While hiring a specialized UX librarian might be useful up to a point, libraries must foster a systemic culture in which all personnel consider how their individual work contributes to the mission of the library and impacts users (Schmidt, 2011). Librarians too often guess or otherwise recommend what we would like for our users, but we really need to consider their needs rather than designing websites and search tools for ourselves.

Some practical suggestions for integrating UX into ASER design would be to (1) conduct usability tests and other direct observation of users while interacting with library webpages and search tools; (2) meet with focus groups of users and/ or specific types of users, e.g., first-year students who use academic libraries; and (3) provide convenient means for users to give just-in-time feedback on websites with carefully placed links, comment fields, and brief online surveys. Finally, iterative design is another aspect to consider when developing tools that benefit users. Consider creating an alternative library website or electronic resources portal for testing by users. Introduce small changes to users during an extended period of testing. Small changes in design can sometimes have a big impact on users.

SUMMARY

While all libraries share the basic function of providing information services to their users, each library needs to consider its own unique resources when crafting a comprehensive ASER with appropriate access and discovery tools. Consider what is affordable now and in the near future and what can be maintained by library personnel. Perhaps your library can afford an e-resource portal and create browsing lists but cannot afford a discovery service. Carefully consider issues of web design, branding, and overall usability. Setting up these tools is not simply a technical question; library personnel must also ensure that users are aware of all of the library's online access tools, how to use these tools properly, and how to get help if they encounter problems.

Responsibility for the development and maintenance of online access tools varies among libraries, but all libraries need to develop the best possible service. Having selected appropriate tools, or at least the best tools available, it is important for librarians to remember the purpose of these tools and what libraries need to do. We are competing with other information services and need to focus on how users actually find information (Dixon et al., 2010). The general principles (see sidebar) should provide some guidance for developing a successful ASER regardless of what specific online access tools are chosen.

GENERAL PRINCIPLES FOR DEVELOPING A SUCCESSFUL ASER

Provide quality metadata

All resource records in all systems should be as accurate and complete as possible. Accurate titles, coverage dates, URLs, and resource description are essential.

Ensure convenience for the user

Webpages, portals, and other tools should be designed for the benefit of the end user, not librarians.

Simplicity is best

Both as a matter of web design, but also in text, messages, resource description, and so on. Use clear, concise language and make everything as simple as possible. Some explanations and some tools will remain necessarily complex, but everything that can be simplified should be simplified.

Eliminate all unnecessary steps to access content

Review how users navigate library webpages and make it as simple as possible to start accessing content.

Make branding ubiquitous

Make sure to brand every electronic resource possible with the name, logo, or symbols of the library or institution. In these times of restricted and declining budgets, it is even more important that every user knows that the library is paying for and providing access to electronic resources.

Solicit feedback

Make it easy for users to get help and provide feedback. Provide links for comments and suggestions on library webpages. Provide contact information for electronic resources professionals and other library personnel as appropriate. Make it very clear that tech support is available.

Make assessments

Gather usage statistics (for library personnel and users) using the best tools available, track page hits and other activity on library webpages, consider consulting with users, conducting usability studies, and taking surveys.

REFERENCES

Becker, B. W. 2009. "Subject Guides 2.0: A Look at LibGuides and Jing." *Behavioral & Social Sciences Librarian* 28, no. 4: 206–209.

Bivens-Tatum, Wayne. 2010. "Imagination, Sympathy, and the User Experience." *Library Journal* 135 (November): 8.

Breeding, Marshall. 2009. "Next Generation Library Automation: Its Impact on the Serials Community." *Serials Librarian* 56, no. 1-4: 55–64.

———. 2010. "The State of the Art in Library Discovery 2010." *Computers in Libraries* 30, no. 1 (January): 31–34.

Brubaker, Noah, Susan Leach-Murray, and Sherri Parker. 2011. "Shapes in the Cloud." *Online* 35, no. 2: 20–26.

Corbett, Lauren E. 2006. "Serials: Review of the Literature 2000–2003." *Library Resources & Technical Services* 50, no. 1: 16–30.

Dixon, Lydia, Cheri Duncan, Jody Condit Fagan, Meris Mandernach, and Stefanie E. Warlick. 2010. "Finding Articles and Journals via Google Scholar, Journal Portals, and Link Resolvers: Usability Study Results." *Reference & User Services Quarterly* 50, no. 2: 170–181.

Ellis, Lisa A., Joseph Hartnett, and Michael Waldman. 2008. "Building Bearcat." *Library Journal* 133 (Summer NetConnect issue): 6–8.

Gall, Dan. 2010. "Librarian Like a Rock Star: Using Your Personal Brand to Promote Your Services and Reach Distant Users." *Journal of Library Administration* 50, no. 5/6: 628–637.

Hassenzahl, Marc, and Noam Tractinsky. 2006. "User Experience—A Research Agenda." *Behaviour & Information Technology* 25, no. 2: 91–97.

Hutchens, Chad. 2011. "Journal Title Transfers: The Process, the Complexities, the Problems, and What the Transfer and KBART Working Groups Are Doing to Address Them." *Serials Librarian* 61, no. 3/4 (October): 389–395.

Linoski, Alexis, and Tine Walczyk. 2008. "Federated Search 101." *Library Journal* 133 (Summer NetConnect issue): 2–5.

Mi, J., Paula Sullenger, and Pat Loghry. 2006. "Examining Workflows and Redefining Roles: Auburn University and the College of New Jersey." *Serials Librarian* 50, no. 3/4: 279–283.

Miksa, Shawne D. 2009. "Resource Description and Access (RDA) and New Research Potentials." *Bulletin of the American Society for Information Science & Technology* 35, no. 5: 47–51.

Rather, Lucia J., and Beacher Wiggins. 1989. "Henriette D. Avram: Close-Up on the Career of a Towering Figure in Library Automation and Bibliographic Control." *American Libraries* 20, no. 9 (October): 855–859.

Schmidt, Aaron. 2011. "Ready for a UX Librarian?" *Library Journal* 136, no. 18 (November): 24.

Tennant, Roy. 2002. "MARC Must Die." *Library Journal* 127, no. 17 (October): 26.

Vaughan, J. 2011a. "Chapter 3: Serials Solutions Summon." *Library Technology Reports* 47, no. 1: 22–29.

———. 2011b. "Chapter 5: Ex Libris Primo Central." *Library Technology Reports* 47, no. 1: 39–47.

Wakimoto, Jina Choi. 2009. "Scope of the Library Catalog in Times of Transition." *Cataloging & Classification Quarterly* 47, no. 5 (July): 409–426.

Wisniewski, Jeff. 2010. "Web Scale Discovery: The Future's So Bright, I Gotta Wear Shades." *Online* 34, no. 4 (July): 55–57.

Chapter Six

Gathering, Evaluating, and Communicating Statistical Usage Information for Electronic Resources

Geoffrey Timms

W hen evaluating e-resources, it is essential to take a close look at the useful- ness patrons derive from them compared to the investment in purchasing or licensing them. While anecdotal evidence of value can, and should, be gathered by talking with those who use the e-resources, decision makers often require more concrete information, namely usage data. The primary focus of this chapter is to consider the process of gathering usage-related data and using it effectively and responsibly to assist in the decision-making process about renewing or discontinu- ing e-resource subscriptions. For the purpose of this chapter, the term "usage data" refers to the raw numbers, provided by the vendor or gathered from an e-resource delivery system, related to the use of an e-resource. The term "usage statistics" refers to numbers or indicators that are generated by processing usage data.

THE NATURE OF USAGE DATA AND STATISTICS

In considering the nature of usage data and statistics, a librarian should reflect upon their reliability. The usage data obtained and statistics generated, and upon which library acquisitions decisions are based, are assumed to be both factual and accurate. However, there are subtle variations in the flavor of truth. Mark Twain (2006), attributing his quotation to British Prime Minister Benjamin Disraeli, stated in his *Chapters from My Autobiography*, "There are three kinds of lies: lies, damned lies, and statistics" (p. 471). This quotation is included here to remind the reader that statistics are not the final word when it comes to evaluating e-resources and that the library community should not allow itself to be subservient to mere dispassionate numbers. They must be interpreted with care and in context so that the conclusion reflects the truth rather than inadvertently purveying a lie.

The march toward electronic holdings of, or access to, materials has accelerated in pace since electronic resources became a viable alternative to print. The *Association of Research Libraries Statistics 2007–2008* report demonstrates the accelerating investment in electronic resources as a percentage of total materials expenditure in a sample of libraries. This percentage grew from 3.6 percent in 1992/1993 to 51.46 percent in 2007/2008 (Kyrillidou and Bland, 2009). The significance of electronic resources in libraries is indisputable, as their accessibility, along with all of the technological innovations that enhance their retrieval, renders them very convenient in an academic environment where nontraditional education structures are blossoming (Bower and Mee, 2010).

As library managers prepare budgets each year, the ever-inflating portion of the budget devoted to e-resources, even in times of a near-static quantity of e-resources in some libraries, must surely have captured the attention of senior administrators. Flemming-May and Grogg (2010) remind the reader that, especially in the current economic climate, "librarians are charged with demonstrating the cost-effectiveness of their services and resources as well as their effective management of the financial resources with which they have been entrusted" (p. 5). This includes the preparation and analysis of indicators of use, accompanied by recommendations for future action. Making recommendations, supported by evidence, is a key activity for the librarian. Perhaps the greatest question asked in relation to e-resources is, "Are they meeting the needs of our patrons?" This question is equally applicable to the discovery and authentication mechanisms by which they are accessed. An underlying assumption seems to exist that relevance equates to use, and therefore results in the familiar question, "How much are they being used?"

Several e-resource practitioners identify numerous problems associated with the generation and analysis of usage data. Henle (2007) highlights three factors that impact the gathering and processing of usage data: "The external aspects are the evolution of standards and technology while the internal aspect is the institution within which the ER librarian operates" (p. 278). All three of these factors are likely to be changing and, on the whole, beyond the control of the librarian. In a 2006 survey of research libraries, great diversity was reported in the amount of time invested in gathering and processing usage data. An average of several weeks a year is fairly typical (Baker and Read, 2008).

Plaguing the integrity of e-resource usage data have been the variations between vendors in the definitions of key usage concepts including session, search, and full-text download. This has become compounded over the years as more and more publishers have begun providing online access to their content, increasing the disparity of these definitions and the consequent generation of usage data (Chisman, 2008). As the diversity of digitized or born-digital monographs has increased, the data provided by vendors, such as ebrary, NetLibrary, and Books24x7, to represent the use of e-books has become quite variable, making comparative evaluations challenging (Sprague and Hunter, 2008). Indeed, underlying the very concept of usage, as demonstrated by usage data, is the assumption that each article or e-book accessed is actually used to some level of significance rather than merely given but a passing glance (Levine-Clark, 2006). Such a quandary is not new to libraries, as similar assumptions have existed about print usage data for a long time.

The development of standards in the generation of usage data is one of the great achievements paralleling the online delivery of scholarly materials. Differences between the techniques used to generate usage data by various vendors have rendered similarly named data sets somewhat incomparable. Such an issue has not gone unnoticed in the e-resource industry. Since 2002 Project COUNTER (Counting Online Usage of Networked Electronic Resources, www.projectcounter.org) has made great strides in developing data standards for documenting e-resource usage, and these standards are increasingly being adopted by publishers and vendors of e-resources. The third release of the *COUNTER Code of Practice for Journals and Databases* includes clear definitions of some of the critical events that generate usage data, such as a session, a search, a successful request, and a turnaway (COUNTER, 2008). The code describes the standards for presenting usage data in great detail, and guidelines for vendors, along with detailed testing requirements, help to ensure that COUNTER-compliant vendors are achieving and maintaining the necessary standards (COUNTER, 2011b). Appendixes B and C in this book present lists of COUNTER-compliant vendors for the third release of the *COUNTER Code of Practice for Journals and Databases* and the first release of the *COUNTER Code of Practice for Books and Reference Works*, respectively, demonstrating which COUNTER reports they provide. Current lists of COUNTER-compliant vendors and the reports they offer can be found at www.projectcounter.org/compliantvendors.html.

Even COUNTER-compliant data are not completely homogeneous, however. While COUNTER definitions of what constitutes a search and a session are robust, Blecic, Fiscella, and Wiberley (2007) note of the second release of the *COUNTER Code of Practice for Journals and Databases* that the auditing specifications leave a little flexibility in counting specific events such as searches that generate no results. This is also true of the third release. The audit specifications themselves acknowledge a requirement of between –8 percent and +2 percent accuracy, for example, to pass audit test DB1-1 (COUNTER, 2011a).

New technologies in the delivery of electronic resources also have the capacity to influence usage data. In their study of three years worth of usage data, Blecic, Fiscella, and Wiberley (2007) propose that federated searching and search alert services both have an impact upon usage metrics such as searches per session. An increase in the number of sessions logged due to the introduction of federated search engines (which can trigger a new session for each search) will reduce the searches-per-session metric. To remain COUNTER compliant, vendors have begun to separate federated and automated session and search data from selective user-initiated session and search data in Database Reports 1 and 3, reflecting the latest *COUNTER Code of Practice* release (COUNTER, 2008), and demonstrating a recognition that such information is of importance to those who evaluate their products. As is typical, however, the development and uptake of standards has a significant time delay across an industry, and consistent treatment of current variations will not likely be achieved for some years.

A variety of inherent e-resource data issues exist, ranging from platform and technical issues to user behavior, all of which affect the generation of usage statistics for decision making. Acknowledging that these issues exist is a key step in developing a strategy to utilize usage data (Nagra, 2009). A particular platform-related issue of concern is that of double-counting full-text article downloads where articles are available in both Hypertext Markup Language (HTML) and Portable Document Format (PDF) versions and where interfaces necessitate the viewing of the HTML article before an option to access a PDF version can be reached (Davis and Price, 2006). This is not always forced, however. ProQuest, WilsonWeb, and EBSCOhost all present HTML full text, where available, when a title link is chosen from a results list despite having individual icons pre-

QUICK TIP

Bear the following guidelines in mind when dealing with usage data:

- Be aware of the limitations and imperfections embodied in usage data.

- Identify what is important to measure and within the department's capacity to process.

- Communicate the data and statistics clearly, acknowledging the imperfections that affect their comparability and interpretation.

sented for HTML and PDF full text (if available) documents in the results list. A user clicking on the title, but seeking PDF format, would likely view both formats. Davis and Price (2006), in their statistical analysis of ratios between PDF and HTML downloads among COUNTER-compliant publishers, propose that variations in full-text access options between publisher platforms affects full-text usage reporting and go on to suggest that a system of weighting full-text usage data to account for interface biases might improve data comparability.

Davis and Price's (2006) proposal, along with Nagra's (2009) outline of numerous quantitative methods for the evaluation of e-resources, brings the attention back to Henle's (2007) consideration of the local institutional environment where two important factors are identified: local valuation of (importance ascribed to) specific data items and the institutional capacity to devote resources to the gathering and evaluation of usage data. In a survey of library consortium members in South Africa, a lack of homogeneity was found in the selection and use of standardized usage data. Attributable to numerous reasons, the authors note that awareness of data standards was not complete across all libraries, and the capacity to devote time to data gathering and processing was also an issue (Dean and de Jager, 2009). Large institutions may have sufficient capacity to devote a full-time position to collection evaluation, but the reality for smaller libraries is that such evaluation is merely one of a host of tasks for a librarian whose responsibilities may span both public and technical services, and even library systems work.

CHOOSING WHICH USAGE DATA TO GATHER

At what point can an e-resource be considered to have been used? When a user opens a database or the interface within which an e-journal is accessed? When the user conducts a search of that e-journal or database, hoping it contains relevant material? When the user reads article abstracts, anticipating that some will provide the desired information? When the user views and/or downloads full-text articles, satisfied in the belief that he or she has been successful in the quest for information? It seems that the user proceeds through different phases during the search for information: hope (choosing a database, book, or e-journal collection in which to search), anticipation (searching and browsing the search results), and satisfaction (selection of full-text articles/books/chapters, if successful). Librarians must consider which of these is the most meaningful to attempt to measure empirically.

When preparing to begin gathering usage data for e-resources, librarians must ask themselves what information they wish to accumulate. The potential data available varies widely by vendor, with some of the small providers of the more obscure publications occasionally providing no data whatsoever. The type of data available also varies by the type of e-resource a librarian is evaluating. Databases, for example, may have data available at the platform, database, or journal title levels. E-journals may have data available at the platform, collection, or journal title levels. Individual e-books may have data available at the title or chapter levels, while e-book collections like ebrary also offer data at the subject area, collection, or platform level. Platforms, like ScienceDirect, may offer access to both e-books and e-journals. Some e-resources, such as NAXOS Music Library, deliver streaming music tracks, whereas others, like ARTstor and H. W. Wilson's Cinema Image Gallery, are databases of images. Such resources have their own unique data items to describe their use, and a librarian must choose which have the most meaning.

Bearing in mind that librarians are interested in deciding whether or not to renew an e-resource on a yearly basis, the data gathered should support that decision at the appropriate acquisition level. In other words, when looking at one of numerous databases from a particular vendor with a common platform, like EBSCOhost, a librarian might be most interested in data at the database level. Gathering data for individual journal titles makes the most sense when the ability exists to make acquisition decisions on a title-by-title basis. If, however, it is important to analyze the use of an e-journal collection, such as SAGE Premier, in detail to understand which titles are being most used and to judge whether it is more efficient to maintain the collection or to subscribe to some of the most-used journals individually, then an evaluator needs to explore usage at the journal title level. While some e-resources are nonstandard insomuch as they do not deliver information in book or journal article form, but rather as images or streaming media, the majority deliver text-based information. Vendors typically provide the following usage data items, or some variation thereof for nonstandard e-resources:

- Sessions: The session count is the number of times the user population accessed a particular resource in the hope of finding what they were looking for within a certain time frame. A session often commences when the user first enters the e-resource but may end in different ways. In some cases a session is only registered when search activity first occurs. Sessions conclude when users exit the e-resource, when browsers crash, or when timeouts are invoked due to periods of no keyboard/mouse activity. Thus, a user may initiate more than one session to accomplish a single task. This could suggest that the more sessions logged, the higher the regard or hope the library's users have that this resource can meet their information needs.

- Searches: The number of times users interacted with this resource in anticipation of finding what they were looking for. Each search can be executed in multiple ways, including the expression of a query in an online form or by using predefined searches in the form of hyperlinked words that are offered as potential search terms or subject descriptors by the interface. Searches may not originate strictly within the e-resource platform but might, for example, be generated by using a search widget on a subject guide. Refinement of searches, including adjusting date ranges, may generate additional search data. Remember that searches may be triggered and counted differently among multiple e-resources. The more searches, the more confidence the librarian can have that users believe they can find information that is useful to them in this resource.

- Full-text downloads: The number of times a user successfully accessed the content he or she found. The definition of full text can vary according to the type of content. It could be a complete journal article, a correction to a journal article, a letter to the editor, a book chapter, a portion of a book chapter, or even a complete book. This could suggest that the number of full-text downloads represents the number of times users believed they had found something relevant to what they were looking for. The more full-text downloads, the more useful material users found, demonstrating the value of this resource. This data is sometimes broken down by format, usually HTML and PDF.

- Turnaways: The number of times a user tried to access this resource but was denied entrance because the maximum concurrent user limit had been reached. A high number of turnaways demonstrates that this resource is in demand, at times, beyond the current authorized level of simultaneous access and that the librarian may need to extend the license to allow access for more simultaneous users.

Another factor that influences which data items are gathered is the type of statistics and assessments that are desired. As the reader will see in a later section of this chapter, Using the Data and Creating Meaningful Statistics, a number of statistics are calculated from two data items. If a librarian wants to calculate the number of searches conducted per user session, then he or she will need to accumulate data for both the number of searches conducted and the number of sessions initiated for each e-resource. Other data will not be available in the same location as usage data. For example, to calculate cost per full-text download, a librarian will need to get the usage data for full-text downloads from the e-resource vendor and subscription cost data from library invoices or financial systems.

The value of usage data can extend beyond the evaluation of the e-resources themselves. Usage data, if available retrospectively, can be used to help assess the effectiveness of library classroom instruction or integrated information literacy instruction (Anderson, 2005). Usage data can show not just how much an e-resource is being used, but how it is being used and from where it is being used. As use is directly related to the ease by which a user can intentionally, or serendipitously, find an e-resource, the point at which a user accesses it is of importance. Use of a key database can be adversely affected if access to it is not available and functioning where the user expects to find it. At Wayne State University, for example, data are drawn from vendor usage data (via Scholarly Stats) as well as other proprietary products/access points, including the A–Z e-journal list, the online catalog, and the electronic resource management system (ERMS), which offer data about e-resource access (Beals and Lesher, 2010). Usage data can also be gathered from other e-resource linking and discovery services such as link resolvers and federated search tools. Coombs (2005) describes SUNY Cortland's 2002 exploration of the value of their proxy server logs to study several elements of e-resource usage, including user decision processes. Data from such services and tools can show from where users reach specific e-resources, which can assist with the marketing thereof.

THE IMPORTANCE OF STANDARDS: COUNTER AND NONSTANDARD USAGE DATA

Perhaps one of the most important considerations in deciding which usage data items to gather is that of standards. When considering the usage data of Springer e-journals alone, for example, standards of data generation may not be at the forefront of an evaluator's mind. When comparing the usage data of Springer e-journals to that of Wiley and Elsevier e-journals, however, such standards become very significant. If data related to full-text usage, for example, were to be calculated differently by Springer compared to Wiley and Elsevier, then a comparison of the three data sets would be of little value because one vendor might have an unfair advantage over the others, possibly giving the impression of superior use. In fact, all three of these vendors are COUNTER compliant with regard to Journal Reports 1 and 1a (see this book's Appendix C).

When using an administrative interface, such as EBSCO or ProQuest Administrator, to access usage data for a given e-resource, it is common to find access to both COUNTER-compliant usage data and other noncompliant usage data. This is due to vendors running parallel usage reporting systems, but also because there is a rather limited, although growing, number of reports available with COUNTER standards. Vendors, therefore, also provide other nonstandard usage data, such as activity by IP address, which facilitates a usage analysis by physical location or by campus affiliation. According to COUNTER's (2011b) compliance guide for vendors, the COUNTER reports that the evaluator can expect to find from a COUNTER-compliant vendor, if they are applicable to the vendor's product, include

- Journal Report 1: Number of successful full-text article requests by month and journal
- Journal Report 1a: Number of successful full-text article requests from an archive by month and journal
- Journal Report 2: Turnaways by month and journal
- Journal Report 5: Number of successful full-text article requests by year and journal
- Database Report 1: Total searches and sessions by month and database
- Database Report 2: Turnaways by month and database
- Database Report 3: Total searches and sessions by month and service
- Consortium Report 1: Number of successful full-text journal article or book chapter requests by month
- Consortium Report 2: Total searches by month and database

The structure of the reports clearly shows the levels at which reporting is available—for individual journal titles, for aggregated databases, and for multi-institution consortia. Guidelines and conditions are provided for other optional reports to be made available at the vendor's discretion, if relevant. COUNTER data that are summarized by year, such as Journal Report 5 as well as the annual totals for the monthly reports, assume a calendar year, unless the reporting interface allows the selection of specific date ranges to include in a report. If a review requires annual totals for an academic year (typically July–June) or any annual cycle other than the calendar year, then Journal Report 5 is of less value, and annual totals for reports where monthly data is provided will have to be calculated for that year. A set of comparable COUNTER standards has been developed for e-books (COUNTER, 2006).

It is important to remember that not all e-resources offer full-text access. Some are purely indexing and abstract products and as such still have great value to researchers. In selecting the data that is of importance, one must not neglect to use data that can be gathered for non-full-text items. Librarians may have fewer options in such cases and must rely primarily on COUNTER session and search data. Sometimes non-COUNTER abstract data may be available and while this cannot identify whether or not the user went on to locate the full-text item, this information can be used it to judge how useful the product may have been.

> **QUICK TIP**
>
> Remember to gather usage data that demonstrates the use of the library's index and abstract databases. These databases can be instrumental in locating articles within the full-text collections, and their value should not be underestimated.

WHEN TO GATHER USAGE DATA

When to gather usage data and prepare it for analysis depends upon the timing of the decision-making process. Two main influences help to determine this decision: the e-resource subscription cycle and the library budget season. If the e-resource subscription runs from July to June, as it does in many academic libraries, then decisions might be made in the spring. Likewise, if a resource is renewed on a calendar-year basis, then the resource would come up for renewal in late fall to early winter. Individual licenses sometimes specify that renewal decisions must be made, for example, 30–60 days before the end of the current license cycle. Budget preparation, however, is often in process as early as six months before its implementation date. Especially in the current economic climate, this necessitates some idea of what the library may be able to afford in the coming fiscal year and may dictate that the library needs to cut a portion of its e-resources. Data will be required to help prioritize e-resources and make the best of potentially difficult decisions.

Knowing how frequently to gather usage data depends upon how current the library's work flows and procedures require it to be for decision making. As the chapter has discussed with COUNTER usage data, monthly data is often the most detailed that is accessible, but nonstandardized data can sometimes be sought with greater granularity, even to the day. For renewal decisions, however, the librarian needs to decide whether to gather usage data monthly, quarterly, semiannually, or annually. Ultimately, it depends upon the timing of decision making. A librarian, for example, with budget decisions being made in November and renewal decisions due in May, as represented by figure 6.1, might choose to use fiscal-year usage data to help formulate budget requests in November and calendar-year usage data in May to assist with renewal decisions. This would provide reasonably current data at both evaluation times and enable comparisons back through the same months in previous years. Data could be gathered monthly and processed semiannually or simply gathered semiannually. When monthly usage data is recorded, custom reports for other time periods can be assembled as needed.

It is worth noting that while many vendors provide usage data for a given month on the first day of the next month, and most by the middle of the next month, platform changes and technical issues can delay the provision of usage data up to two months. Some vendors, like ValueLine, currently provide data only upon request by e-mail. Also, vendors provide retrospective usage data to varying extents. At worst, only the current year's data is maintained. At best, all historical data is available from the very beginning of the subscription. Ultimately, it is up to the individual library to determine how current data must be for decision making. If using data for the last complete calendar year, in the case of the previous example, is acceptable at budget time in November, then there is no need to gather data in July.

Figure 6.1. A Timetable for Semi-Annual Gathering of Usage Data According to Reporting Requirements

Jan	Feb	Mar	Apr	May	Jun	Jul	Aug	Sep	Oct	Nov	Dec

Gather/process calendar-year usage data

Gather/process fiscal-year usage data

Evaluate usage data and make renewal decisions

Evaluate usage data and make budget requests

METHODS FOR GATHERING USAGE DATA

Gathering usage data can be a large undertaking, especially if the library subscribes to a large number of e-resources for which it requires usage data. For institutions with funds for such a service, a number of proprietary products enable the automation of usage data gathering. Chisman (2008) describes one such service from Swets, called Scholarly Stats, and outlines her experiences implementing it and integrating it with other services such as Innovative Interface's Electronic Resource Management module at Washington State University. Of note is the amount of up-front time investment and library systems adjustments necessary to achieve full integrated functionality. A recent initiative, Pubget (http://pubget.com), which streamlines the search and retrieval of PDF documents accessible to institutions with interest in the biomedical field, offers subscriptions to a usage data management tool, PaperStats. The University of Southern California Norris Medical Library worked as a beta tester with Pubget to develop and refine PaperStats following their implementation of Pubget. PaperStats retrieves COUNTER-compliant usage data from vendors, facilitating assessment and comparison (Curran, 2011). Curran notes that during beta testing, some vendors were persuaded to begin production of COUNTER-compliant usage data. PaperStats in now out of beta testing and is available on a subscription model (PRWeb, 2011).

The automation of usage data gathering is possible primarily thanks to another relatively recent standard known as the Standardized Usage Statistics Harvesting Initiative (SUSHI). Developed by members of the National Information Standards Organization (NISO) and working closely with major e-resource providers and Project COUNTER since 2005 (NISO, 2005), SUSHI, "defines an automated request and response model for the harvesting of electronic resource usage data utilizing a Web services framework" (NISO, 2011). Users of products that employ SUSHI must invest time initially to configure their accounts with the information necessary to access the usage data of each e-resource to which they subscribe. After an initial time-consuming effort, the benefit is enjoyed of having a single interface to access COUNTER-quality usage data and the added advantage of proprietary report generation tools.

For institutions unable to invest in subscription services or in internal development to automate the collection of usage data, there is the manual data-gathering method, which can be laborious each time data is gathered. Each vendor's administrative interface must be accessed, reports requested and generated, and data downloaded and organized into a useful format. However, many vendors, like

EBSCO, do facilitate the delivery of usage data by e-mail. The evaluator simply has to identify the desired report(s), choose an output format, and provide a valid e-mail address, and then usage data will arrive via e-mail, usually monthly. In some cases this is established automatically when a subscription is begun. Sometimes usage data can be delivered as attachments. EBSCO delivers a URL that links straight to the appropriate report. Sometimes a vendor will offer the option to download reports in a number of different formats. WilsonWeb offers output in comma-separated values (CSV), HTML, text, or Extensible Markup Language (XML) formats. CSV and tab-delimited downloads are particularly useful for easy transfer to spreadsheet software.

To improve efficiency in gathering usage data, it pays to be systematic. Ensure that for a given vendor the library staff only logs in to the administrative interface once and gathers all the available data for each product or title at that time. To facilitate ease of launching and authenticating with the administrative interfaces, keep a spreadsheet or database of log-in URLs and passwords and work steadily down that list, hyperlinking straight to the interface and copying and pasting usernames and passwords into the log-in screen. This also helps to reduce the possibility that a resource will be missed due to human error. Naturally, the security of these files is important. It is wise to password-protect the file containing the list of sensitive information and ensure that it is not widely available on the network.

CHALLENGES AND PITFALLS: WHAT DOES USAGE DATA REALLY REPRESENT?

In the ideal context of a library where all e-resources are subscribed with access available for all possible users, some of the following considerations are not points of concern. If the library is like many smaller academic libraries, where the diverse information needs of the community are coupled with small populations and budgets, then e-resource licensing is a significant financial challenge, especially with expensive specialized scholarly resources. Many libraries strive to make access to all resources available to all users, but the reality is that some e-resources, such as those used in law, medicine, or other more specific and unique content areas, are relevant only to specific user populations and the cost of making them universally available is prohibitive. So on occasion, databases are licensed for specific locations or for a smaller subset of users, rather than for the whole library system. The usage data gathered about such e-resources, then, carries with it the caveat that it does not represent university-wide usage, but only that of a specific subset of the population. This introduces issues of comparability of usage data.

Similarly, the librarian tries to make e-resources available to library users wherever they are, often by means of proxy servers which enable users from outside of the library's network to access subscription resources by an authentication process. Most, although not all, publishers allow off-site access to their e-resources. So data gathered about these specific journals' usage represents on-campus usage only. This is significant, because with increasing use of resources by nontraditional students and with ever-increasing home computer ownership, more and more people want to access e-resources remotely. If an e-resource is not made available remotely, its usage may be much lower than if it were. While some might consider lower usage a legitimate strike against such a restrictive license clause, it does not lessen the importance of the resource to its community.

Considering library discovery tools—link resolvers, federated search engines, online catalogs, and discovery layers—the presence of an e-resource in each of these services increases its potential use. Yet some e-resources are not included in all of the library's discovery services (services used to search the entirety of a library's content regardless of format or location), either by choice or due to their unique peculiarities that render them incompatible. As with off-campus restrictions on some e-resources, exclusion from discovery services reduces the successful direct, cross-linking, or serendipitous discovery of that e-resource. Usage data will not reflect the cases where usage might or would have occurred, if only it had been accessible within a specific discovery tool.

CHECKLIST: WHAT DOES MY USAGE DATA REPRESENT?

❑ Does this data span a complete year of use?

❑ How much of the user population is able to use this e-resource?

❑ Can it be accessed remotely?

❑ Can it, or its content, be discovered in all the same locations as other e-resources (catalog, A–Z list, subject guides, link resolver, etc.)?

❑ Is it searchable by and included in a federated search tool?

The librarian or other evaluator must remember this unseen condition that is carried with the data.

Of special note is the influence of consortia in the acquisition of e-resources. Libraries depend increasingly upon participation in consortia to maximize their access to e-resources. Depending upon the vendor and consortium, usage data may or may not be available with granularity at the institution or campus levels. Some consortia, such as Georgia's statewide virtual library GALILEO (GeorgiA LIbrary LEarning Online), have developed and refined comprehensive usage data reporting tools to homogenize usage reports generated by numerous participating vendors and, in the case of GALILEO, "They provide an objective measurement of the success of the initiative and individual resources" (GALILEO, 2011).

ORGANIZING USAGE DATA

Particularly true for those who must download usage data manually, but also relevant to those who want to combine numerous usage reports, the organization of the data requires careful planning. For many, Microsoft Excel will be the software of choice for organizing usage data and for generating reports. Capable of multipage spreadsheets and intersheet and interfile dependency, and with a multitude of tools, Microsoft Excel offers the functionality and flexibility to create comprehensive data structures.

In creating complex structures for the storage and use of data, efficiency is a high priority. Each data item should only be entered into the spreadsheet in one place, and all calculations and references to that data item should be performed using the calculating power of spreadsheet formulae and cell referencing. The simple reason for this is that the library staff should only have to add or change data in one location rather than in several different places. A change made in that one location will automatically replicate through all references to that location and the results of all formulae referencing that location will automatically be recalculated when the data is updated. A well-designed spreadsheet structure requires a significant amount of forethought, but the benefits are reaped when populating the data entry portion automatically generates the statistics upon which the librarian will, at least in part, base decisions.

Consider, for example, the data entry sheet of a multipage spreadsheet for vendor-provided database usage data as shown in table 6.1. Data is provided with monthly granularity for each resource and several data points are gathered. Session, search, and full-text download data (where applicable) are manually downloaded and recorded, as well as turnaways with maximum simultaneous users noted for reference. Monthly data is totaled for the fiscal year, and totals for the previous two years are also included by referencing previous years' sheets. In addition, cost data

Table 6.1. A Sample Data Entry Page of a Usage Data Spreadsheet

	A	B	C	D	E	F	G	H	I	J	K	L	M	N	O	P	Q
	Name	Data Type	Jul	Aug	Sep	Oct	Nov	Dec	Jan	Feb	Mar	Apr	May	Jun	FY10	FY09	FY08
1	DB1	Price													$5,120	$5,040	$4,800
2																	
3		Sessions	804	329	2,586	2,783	3,547	3,846	903	3,445	3,597	4,867	1,945	1,812	30,464	29,045	24,944
4		Searches	1,116	441	3,290	3,458	4,689	4,667	1,221	4,223	4,697	6,006	2,540	2,325	38,673	37,998	31,036
5		Full Text	2,896	501	8,491	8,643	12,541	12,981	1,989	11,473	12,911	16,727	3,024	2,946	95,123	42,895	29,056
6		Max. users	N/A	N/A	N/A	N/A	N/A	N/A	N/A	N/A	N/A	N/A	N/A	N/A	N/A	N/A	N/A
7		Turnaways	N/A	N/A	N/A	N/A	N/A	N/A	N/A	N/A	N/A	N/A	N/A	N/A	N/A	N/A	N/A
8																	
9	DB2	Price													$4,300	$4,100	$3,900
10		Sessions	626	225	1,249	1,680	2,944	2,866	421	1,296	2,421	2,986	1,709	1,775	20,198	23,245	24,129
11		Searches	887	296	1,225	2,126	3,296	3,145	559	1,319	3,161	3,414	2,196	2,234	23,858	24,946	26,492
12		Full Text	505	125	621	1,113	1,494	1,507	335	741	1,212	1,456	1,171	1,419	11,699	12,889	14,451
13		Max. users	N/A	N/A	N/A	N/A	N/A	N/A	N/A	N/A	N/A	N/A	N/A	N/A	N/A	N/A	N/A
14		Turnaways	N/A	N/A	N/A	N/A	N/A	N/A	N/A	N/A	N/A	N/A	N/A	N/A	N/A	N/A	N/A
15																	
16	DB3	Price													$2,850	$2,575	$2,450
17		Sessions	79	44	219	221	296	314	84	312	325	396	156	161	2,607	2,420	1,991
18		Searches	102	69	304	200	391	396	141	521	491	485	184	179	3,463	3,134	1,450
19		Full Text	96	52	359	245	496	456	161	758	602	571	196	144	4,136	3,963	1,695
20		Max. users	6	6	6	6	6	6	6	6	6	6	6	6	6	2	2
21		Turnaways	0	0	2	12	8	6	0	3	7	6	0	0	44	289	185

is included for the current and previous two years. It is within this sheet that data is consolidated from various vendor sources, and this data is referenced in other sheets to generate usage statistics, as the reader shall see later.

USING THE DATA AND CREATING MEANINGFUL STATISTICS

The library staff can use downloaded usage data as is, ascribing meaning to it, and can also create usage statistics or metrics. Usage statistics are generated by combining two, sometimes more, available data items to express the concepts that they are believed to represent, in numerical terms. This may include not only vendor-provided data but also institutional data. The following statistics are popular:

Searches per Session

This data can be described as the average number of searches conducted per session. The more searches per session, the more frequently users interacted with this resource. An average of zero searches per session suggests they came and did nothing. An average of one search per session either means they tried once, failed, and left; or it may mean they came, tried, and succeeded the first time. Many searches per session may either mean ongoing success or, at least, persistence in trying to find what they needed despite having difficulty.

Full-Text Downloads per Session

The average number of full-text downloads per session. The number of relevant items users found, on average, per visit. The more the resource found per session, the more successful it was.

Full-Text Downloads per Search

The average number of full-text downloads per search. The number of relevant items users found, on average, per search. The more the resource found, the more efficient they were each time they searched.

Cost per Search

The average cost per search conducted by users. The higher the number of searches conducted, the lower the cost per search. So a relatively low cost per search is, in theory, good.

Cost per Full-Text Download

The average cost per successful full-text document retrieval by users. The higher the number of successful downloads, the lower the cost per download, so lower is good. Cost per full-text download is a particularly useful statistic when contemplating a transition to a pay-as-you-go subscription model or when analyzing e-journal use compared to interlibrary loan costs.

Percentage Change

Applicable to any data item, percentage changes demonstrate relative increases or decreases in data over time. Key data items to track with percentage changes over time are cost, search, and full-text download data.

Per Capita Data

Analyzing any data item in the context of the size of the user population (e.g., cost per capita or searches per capita) can provide useful information. Generated by dividing cost or use, for example, by the full-time equivalent (FTE) count, per capita data demonstrates the average cost or use per potential user. It is important to use an FTE count of people who actually have access to the e-resource. Per capita statistics for specialized e-resources such as chemistry or music databases can be analyzed using the FTE of those specific departments and could be useful during budget negotiations. In settings where an FTE is not available, a user population head count is appropriate.

Table 6.2. A Spreadsheet of Calculated Usage Statistics

	A	B	C	D	E	F	G	H	I	J	K
1	Name	Full Text?	Searches FY08	Searches FY09	+/- %	Searches FY10	+/- %	Current Searches/ Session	Current FT Views/ Search	Current $ per Search	Current $ per FT Viewed
2	DB1	Y	31,036	37,998	22.43%	38,673	1.78%	1.27	2.46	$0.13	$0.05
3	DB2	Y	26,492	24,946	-5.84%	23,858	-4.36%	1.18	0.49	$0.18	$0.37
4	DB3	Y	1,450	3,134	116.14%	3,463	10.50%	1.33	1.19	$0.82	$0.69

SPREADSHEET CALCULATIONS

Usage statistics can be calculated and presented on a separate sheet from the data entry sheet, directly referencing cells in the data entry sheet. An example of a Database Calculated Statistics sheet is shown in table 6.2, where raw search data is directly referenced and reproduced in the table and calculated data is produced by referencing raw data with the formulae. In this Excel sheet, a direct reference to the FY08 search data for DB1 in the sheet named Data Entry Page (see table 6.1) is made with this formula:

='Data Entry Page'!Q4

The calculated Current $ per Full Text Viewed statistic for DB1 is calculated using this formula:

='Data Entry Page'!O2/'Data Entry Page'!O5

The percentage change in searches between FY09 and FY10 for DB1 references data within the current (Calculated Usage Statistics) sheet and is presented in a cell with the data type formatted as a percentage and calculated with this formula:

=(F2-D2)/D2

STRENGTHS AND WEAKNESSES OF STATISTICS

Statistics are only as good as the data from which they are generated. The librarian must remember the weaknesses of the raw usage data provided by vendors and consider the impact this may have upon some popular statistics.

Session data may be inflated due to federated searching. If a librarian has previously assumed that a session represented a conscious decision by a user to search an e-resource one or more times, then he or she can no longer maintain this perspective in the knowledge that a new session is documented for a given e-resource every time a user conducts a federated search. As previously suggested, this will reduce the searches per session statistic. Similarly, this will lower the cost per session statistic, suggesting greater cost effectiveness than is perhaps true.

Federated searching, however, may also lend itself to boosting search counts in resources that users would not typically have chosen. Coombs (2005) noted surprise at how few of SUNY Cortland's databases were individually being selected by users to search, according to EZProxy logs. Depending upon the configuration of a federated search tool and which databases are included in searches, otherwise neglected databases may be searched more often, albeit inadvertently, by users of the federated search when it is introduced. If this is true then search data will increase, with session data increasing at a similar rate. Both of these data influences, especially in institutions where federated searching is popular, will cause a searches per session statistic to gravitate toward a value of one (Blecic, Fiscella, and Wiberley, 2007). Similarly, any unintentional searching of irrelevant databases included in a federated search will boost search data counts. All increases in search data, legitimate or artificial, will cause the cost per search statistic to appear more favorable.

The issue of double-counting full-text downloads in interfaces that automatically display HTML versions of documents while users actually go on to select PDF versions for download also impacts popular statistics. Cost per full-text download

> **QUICK TIP:**
> **Enter Each Data Item Only Once**
>
> - To display the same data in a different spreadsheet page, refer to the cells containing the original data using a cell-referencing formula.
>
> - To present the result of a calculation of two or more data items, refer to the cells already containing the data in the formula.
>
> - To further utilize the spreadsheet, generate graphs to represent the data visually.

will be artificially reduced and full-text downloads per search or full-text downloads per session will be artificially increased, both of which favor the vendor that double-counts full-text downloads.

With such knowledge, it is tempting for the evaluator to throw his or her hands in the air in dismay and ask, "What's the point of bothering with usage data?" Instead, it is much more constructive to consider himself or herself armed with valuable insight into the weaknesses of usage statistics and go into the interpretive process with open eyes.

INTERPRETING USAGE DATA AND STATISTICS IN CONTEXT

When interpreting usage data and statistics, it is essential to remember that the numbers, at best, can merely demonstrate *what* happened with regard to the use of a specific e-resource, as logged by the vendor, not *why* it happened. These numbers, with their imperfections, must be interpreted by adding to the mix the knowledge that the librarian has about his or her institution and its users, vendors, and e-resource delivery systems.

Changes in the environments in which libraries and librarians work occur over time, both rapidly and slowly, for the better or for the worse. Academic libraries may experience changes in their FTE counts, representing potential library users. Public libraries may experience demographic shifts in the populations they serve, both in numbers and in makeup. Academic libraries experience changing use as degree programs are added or removed. Institutions increasing their graduate programs may experience significant increases in research emphasis as the graduate student FTE count grows. Law and medical libraries experience additional research interests as new specialty practices are introduced to law firms and hospitals. Public libraries may need to expand their electronic access to news content or electronic book content due to shifts in user populations or current events. There is a danger of focusing solely on the environment that the librarian controls and observes. The reality is that many decisions related to electronic resources are influenced by external factors, for users are driven by external motivators.

Take, for example, the case of an education-specific database in which current usage data shows a significantly increased number of full-text downloads. This high use may be because the education FTE count has grown rapidly and because the institution has added education doctoral programs with their strong research components. Or perhaps the vendor of this education database has changed its interface and is now automatically displaying HTML full-text content when records are opened. Maybe this database has recently been added to the federated search tool. Perhaps the education subject librarian has invested time in showing the education faculty the database and its features. These are just a few of the environmental and technical contextual considerations or variables that may have contributed to the high usage reported. All or some of these could be true.

Case Study: A Premier Subject-Specific E-resource

The following COUNTER-compliant usage data and statistics represent a premier subject-specific e-resource and the context in which it is used:

- Cost: $15,000
- Sessions: 2,207; previous year: 1,722
- Searches: 2,725; previous year: 2,092
- Full-text article downloads: 2,473; previous year: 2,002
- 150 total majors and minors in the subject area
- Six faculty
- Searches/session: 1.24
- Full-text article downloads/search: 0.91
- Cost/full-text article download: $6.07

This e-resource is not included in a federated search utility. Is it being used sufficiently to justify renewal?

Looking at key statistics, a librarian can propose the following:

- The number of searches per session is greater than one. This indicates that, on average, each visitor to this e-resource is conducting at least one search. It is not particularly high, but, on average, there is at least one user interaction, which is positive. The bias toward a value of one due to federated searching does not apply in this case.
- At 0.91 full-text downloads per search, on average, 91 percent of searches result in a full-text article being chosen for download/view. This is a reasonable rate of success.
- The calculated average cost per full-text article downloaded of $6.07 seems alarming at first, but for premier scholarly literature it is somewhat reasonable compared to pay-as-you-go costs.

- Considering the specialized nature of this resource, calculating the number of searches and full-text views per registered student in this subject discipline (18.17 and 16.49, respectively) indicates that it is being well used per capita.
- The three main data items (sessions, searches, and full-text downloads) have all increased by between 23 percent and 30 percent when compared to the previous year's usage data. It would be prudent to verify any possible changes with the vendor's reporting of usage to ensure that these increases reflect actual changes in use.
- Not represented here numerically, an analysis of the research activity of the targeted user group would provide additional information as to the perceived value of this resource.

> **QUICK TIP**
>
> Usage data and statistics can only tell us *what* happened with regard to e-resource usage as logged by the vendor, not *why* it happened. Interpret these numbers, with their imperfections, by adding to the mix knowledge about the library's parent institution, users, vendors, and e-resource delivery systems.

Overall, the data and statistics related to this e-resource suggest a case for renewal.

The Context of Peer Resources: Resource Comparison

The numerous potential variations in usage data, both from the vendor side in terms of data generation and standards and from the local institution in terms of context and what/whose use the data represents, make comparisons between e-resources very challenging. The primary reason to compare two or more resources is likely to be related to deciding whether to renew them all or to drop a subscription. It is important, then, to only make comparisons where the data is legitimately comparable.

Multiple mainstream publishers produce similar scholarly resources, be they e-journals or aggregated databases, that compete directly with each other. Often they have unique features or content, but they also have very much in common (an overlap analysis can help clarify the uniqueness of, and similarities between, several databases). In order to try to compare the usage data related to multiple e-resources, the library staff needs to ensure that

- each is accessible to the same user population or data can be generated for comparable portions of the user population;

- each is accessible in the same places (on and off campus);
- each is discoverable in the same places (A–Z e-journal list, library list of databases, link resolver, federated search, online catalog, etc.);
- each offers similar standardized data points—COUNTER reports; and
- usage data is available for the same date ranges for each e-resource.

Any variation from the above criteria will introduce erroneous reasoning into the decision-making process and result in judgment being made inappropriately. These criteria are reasonably within the librarian's grasp to reconcile. It is the more subtle variations in data generation by e-resource vendors where data discrepancies may occur. While it is possible to engage in detailed statistical analysis of the comparability of different vendors' usage data, this is logistically unrealistic for many smaller libraries to undertake. What can easily be done is to investigate the e-resource interface to check for obvious issues. If one database interface automatically presents the user with the HTML version of an article when opening a record, even though the user intended to proceed to view the PDF, then the full-text usage data cannot legitimately be compared with that of a database that does not display any full-text item before the user makes a choice about the full-text format. Testing for session time-outs is also a legitimate preparatory exercise before interpreting usage data. Some e-resource administrative interfaces permit time-out triggers to be adjusted and, where possible, they should be standardized.

If the usage data for several e-resources is incomparable for reasons mentioned earlier, or if an evaluator is contemplating just one e-resource, then other methods exist for evaluation. One popular technique is to compare the trends among each e-resource's usage data and incorporate this information into the judgment.

The Context of Time: Trends

While the librarian can gain some insight by comparing one resource to another, it is equally important to look at data for a single e-resource over time. In doing so, an evaluator can identify trends that help him or her to understand how successfully it is being used over time and consider the changes in cost-benefit that may have occurred. To identify a trend, a minimum of three years of data is needed, although a longer time span is preferable. This means that data must have been collected for a time before an analysis can occur. It is, therefore, important to plan ahead and secure all potentially needed data for future availability even if current analysis does not utilize every data item gathered.

Trends are an important consideration, particularly true in academic libraries and truer yet for subject-specific e-resources, because of demand cycles. Related to the frequency of course offerings, the demand for access to scholarly material for research by the student body may be cyclical. Some higher level courses may be offered only once every two to three years, and if they have a strong research component, then they can have a significant impact on a specialized subject-specific e-resource. An organic chemistry course may follow the pattern of laboratory work in the fall semester with a research project in the spring semester, giving the impression of low demand for American Chemical Society journals in the fall, but high demand in the spring. Similarly, a surge in research activity by a specific department's faculty can create a temporary period of high use that subsides again after the research is completed. Likewise, public libraries may see an uptick in the usage of electronic collections pertaining to certain hot topics or large national events. One example of this would be the presidential election cycle.

In public libraries, demand for particular electronic resources is based primarily upon the needs of the patrons, which stem not from within the institution, as in academic libraries and their curricular offerings, but from the multitude of environmental factors that influence their need or desire for information. For example, demand for news resources may increase at times when particularly significant events are occurring in the life of a community, a state, or the nation. Disasters, crises, wars, scandals, and celebrations are all occasional situations that can peak interest and fuel the pursuit of further news information. An economic depression may increase interest in education and career resources, as well as demand for information related to economics, small businesses, frugal living, and investments. Events of serious medical significance such as avian influenza, severe acute respiratory syndrome (SARS), and E. coli outbreaks may increase demand for government health resources in MEDLINE. Political research may increase during election campaigns. Corporate libraries may experience a waxing or waning of research interests as the enterprise's business activities diversify or become more targeted.

When looking at trends in the use of e-resources, it is important to try to associate knowledge of the context with any unusual changes in the data. Take, for example, the graph in figure 6.2, which shows session, search, and full-text views usage data for an abstract/full-text database over time. The upturn in full-text downloads from 2008–2009 is associated with the addition of a significant number of full-text titles to the database. A librarian cannot assume the additional full-text content is the sole reason for this upturn because numerous other contextual factors influence the numbers. It is logical, however, to attribute at least

111

some of the increase in full-text downloads to the fact that the database contains more full-text documents than previously. In addition, looking at the accelerated increase in full-text use from 2009–2010, a librarian could assume that patrons were realizing the added value of this database and downloading more full-text documents from it. This, however, does not tie in with the fact that the increase in full-text retrieval was very much higher than the modest increase in sessions and searches. In fact, the vendor adjusted its method of reporting full-text use during this time period, resulting in an apparent increase. A librarian or other evaluator cannot know to what extent the data would have increased (or possibly decreased) in the absence of the vendor's change in reporting behavior. The full-text data for 2009–2010, then, should be considered incomparable to other years due to the change in reporting standards.

Another example of a changing trend is demonstrated by the graph in figure 6.3, which represents Thomson Reuters' Web of Science, an index/abstract database. A significant increase in searches in 2010 coincides with the introduction of several sizable high impact e-journal collections from premier publishers. Previously, verbal reports indicated that the value of the database was unappreciated because after finding relevant citations, very little full-text content could be accessed in the university's e-resource repertoire. The introduction of significant collections of full-text journals in 2009 means that researchers face a much greater probability of being

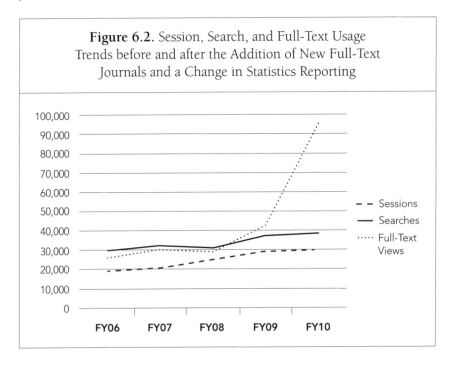

Figure 6.2. Session, Search, and Full-Text Usage Trends before and after the Addition of New Full-Text Journals and a Change in Statistics Reporting

able to pursue searches to completion with a full-text download in one of the new collections. This is reflected in a much higher ratio of searches to sessions in 2010.

Comparing usage trends among e-resources makes up for some of the challenges faced in comparing raw data for those e-resources. For example, while a higher number of searches for one e-resource may suggest its superiority over another, the fact that its use trend has declined over several years while the other shows increased use over the same period can be fairly informative. Figure 6.4 shows data representing searches and full-text downloads for two competing databases. One clearly appears to be used more than the other, but that assumes that the data is strictly comparable. By analyzing the trends, however, it is clear that database DB1 shows an increasing trend in searches and full-text downloads (noting that the 2009–2010 full-text data is to be discounted for the reason outlined previously), while DB2 shows a decreasing trend over time.

The purpose of such analysis is predominantly to draw attention to underutilized e-resources, although it is just as important to demonstrate to administrators that recent investments in new resources are paying off with high use. Once an e-resource has been identified as potentially underutilized, providing insufficient benefit for the money invested in subscribing to it, or of diminishing perceived value, steps must be taken to reach a decision about what action to take. This is where data and context are discussed and a decision is reached to either try to

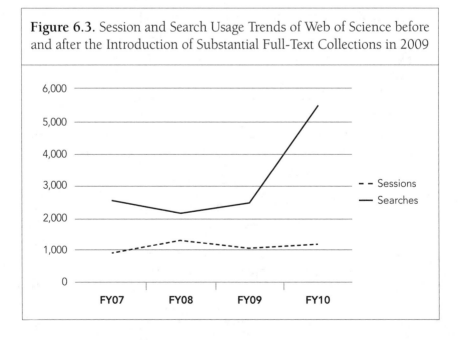

Figure 6.3. Session and Search Usage Trends of Web of Science before and after the Introduction of Substantial Full-Text Collections in 2009

increase usage, gather feedback from the user community, or to proceed with cancellation.

CREATING AND EXPLAINING REPORTS

Why create reports? Cancellation decisions sometimes involve people who are not familiar with usage data, the statistics the librarian generates, or the interpretation thereof. The cancellation of an e-resource can be an inflammatory event, straining the relationship between the library staff and its patrons. It is important, therefore, to be able to communicate and justify the decision in a clear and concise way. A report also provides a history to which the library staff can refer in the future to remind themselves why certain decisions were made. There is a temptation to fill the report with every piece of data available to bolster the justification, but that is likely to render it confusing to the reader. An effective report only needs to contain what must be said to get the message across accurately and convincingly. Librarians must demonstrate that they are not acting with reckless indifference; rather, they must communicate the attention and care that they have invested in interpreting usage data and in making recommendations about the continuance or cessation of e-resource subscriptions.

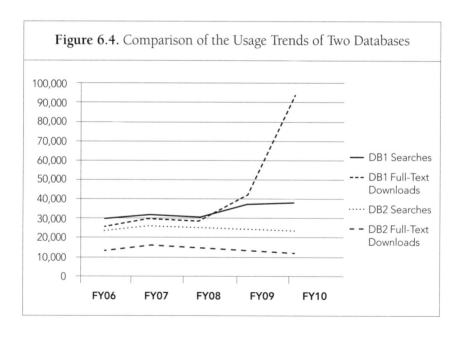

Figure 6.4. Comparison of the Usage Trends of Two Databases

Communicating key statistics in a report requires a clear definition of what the statistics mean to a specific library and in context to a specific information need. If the evaluator has determined, with experience, that a low number of searches per session (fewer than one, for example) is a reliable indicator of the poor usability of an e-resource interface, then that definition should accompany the statistic in the report along with any supporting anecdotal evidence. When trying to demonstrate a trend in usage, graphs are much more effective than tables of data. Data can draw the reader in, trying to make sense of the individual numbers and losing sight of the broad picture. A graph, on the other hand, is a broad-level communicative tool designed to keep the reader focused on the big picture. There are certainly times when numerical data must be presented for analysis, but only when it is truly necessary to do so.

REVIEW AND RENEWAL OR CANCELLATION OF RESOURCES

In order to be fiscally responsible, a librarian may recommend the cancellation of e-resources due to low use or value, even though the library can actually afford to maintain them, preferring to try to license something of greater relevance or utility. In the current challenging economic climate, a librarian may be forced to make cancellation decisions even though he or she does not want to cease subscriptions to any currently subscribed e-resources. In this context the librarian seeks to minimize the negative effect this may have upon the institution's support of its patrons by eliminating the e-resources that will least hinder research activity by their absence.

Equipped with usage reports, anecdotal information, and initial recommendations, the process of review must include feedback from the users of e-resources slated for cancellation. In fact, it is prudent to obtain feedback, both formally and informally, from stakeholders in the user community for e-resources that the librarian still believes to be worth maintaining. As libraries exist to help their patrons meet their information needs, it is important to foster a collaborative atmosphere of partnership in deciding the fate of an e-resource. This is because assumptions can lead to inaccurate conclusions. Based upon usage data, an evaluator may assume that an e-resource is not valued by patrons when in reality some of them might not even be aware they have access to it. In other cases, it might be acceptable to patrons to drop an e-journal subscription when embargoed content (access available except for the current 12 months, for example) is provided in an aggregated database. Perhaps most important, a subscription to a particular e-resource or a certain number of subject-relevant e-resources may be a prerequisite for the accreditation of the school in question. Such information cannot be discerned by acting in isolation.

E-resource renewal decisions are normally due at a specific point in time. Sometimes licenses specify that renewals must be made by the time the subscription cycle concludes, but others may specify that commitment to renew or termination notification must be made one or two months before the end of the subscription period. For this reason, as discussed earlier, the librarian must be aware of license details and ready to make decisions in a timely manner, beginning with the gathering of data and ending with the communication of intent to the e-resource vendor.

SUMMARY

The importance of usage data and statistics in making and justifying e-resource renewal decisions is substantial. The challenges faced in gathering data, creating and processing statistics, and reaching responsible conclusions are ever increasing. Before tackling these challenges, an evaluator must be certain of what he or she wants to achieve and how he or she is willing to tackle it, deciding upon a scale of usage analysis that is meaningful and sustainable in each library's individual context. Making the library and user communities aware of the subtle variations that exist in the definitions of usage between vendors, the attempts to achieve standards, and the nuances of specific data items equip the librarian to use usage data wisely.

> Statistics are not the final word when it comes to evaluating e-resources. The library community should not allow itself to be subservient to the mere dispassionate numbers; rather, statistics must be interpreted with care and in context so that the conclusion does indeed reflect the truth rather than inadvertently purvey a lie.

Once a librarian has decided which data points to document and which statistical indicators are most meaningful, he or she can then embark upon the data-gathering process. Whichever way, however labor-intensive the process of gathering data, an evaluator must ensure that it is stored in a manageable structure from which it can be manipulated and processed efficiently and accurately. Populated according to the timetable that provides up-to-date data at critical decision-making times during the year, the usage data repository can be used to generate specific usage statistics automatically. Armed with the data and statistics, the librarian should resist the temptation to process these numbers into renewal decisions without carefully contemplating the context, adding value to the data with knowledge about the environment in which the e-resources are used. Incorporating input from the primary users of e-resources helps to promote a collaborative environment, reducing errors of assumption and expanding contextual knowledge. In this manner, responsible renewal or cancellation decisions can be made.

REFERENCES

Anderson, Elise. 2005. "Maximizing the Value of Usage Data." *Against the Grain* 17, no. 5: 20–22.

Baker, Gayle, and Eleanor J. Read. 2008. "Vendor-Supplied Usage Data for Electronic Resources: A Survey of Academic Libraries." *Learned Publishing* 21, no. 1: 48–57. doi:10.1087/095315108X247276.

Beals, Nancy, and Marcella Lesher. 2010. "Managing Electronic Resource Statistics." *Serials Librarian* 58, no. 1: 219–223. doi:10.1080/03615261003625844.

Blecic, Deborah D., Joan B. Fiscella, and Stephen E. Wiberley Jr. 2007. "Measurement of Use of Electronic Resources: Advances in Use Statistics and Innovations in Resource Functionality." *College & Research Libraries* 68, no. 1: 26–44.

Bower, Shirley L., and Susan A. Mee. 2010. "Virtual Delivery of Electronic Resources and Services to Off-Campus Users: A Multifaceted Approach." *Journal of Library Administration* 50, no. 5/6: 468–483. doi: 10.1080/01930826.2010.488593.

Chisman, Janet K. 2008. "Electronic Resource Usage Data: Standards and Possibilities." *Serials Librarian* 53, no. 4: 79–89. doi:10.1300/J123v53n04_06.

Coombs, Karen A. 2005. "Lessons Learned from Analyzing Library Database Usage Data." *Library Hi Tech* 23, no. 4: 598–609. doi:10.1108/07378830510636373.

COUNTER (Counting Online Usage of Networked Electronic Resources). 2006. "The COUNTER Code of Practice: Books and Reference Works; Release 1." Project Counter. www.projectcounter.org/cop/books/cop_books_ref.pdf.

———. 2008. "The COUNTER Code of Practice for Journals and Databases: Release 3." Project Counter. www.projectcounter.org/r3/Release3D9.pdf.

———. 2011a. "Code of Practice for Journals and Databases: Release 3; Appendix E; Auditing Requirements and Tests." Project Counter. www.projectcounter.org/r3/r3_E .pdf.

———. 2011b. "COUNTER Compliance: A Step-by-Step Guide for Vendors." Project Counter. www.projectcounter.org/documents/COUNTER_compliance_stepwise_guide.pdf.

Curran, Megan. 2011. "Debating Beta: Considerations for Libraries." *Journal of Electronic Resources in Medical Libraries* 8, no. 2: 117–125.

Davis, Philip M., and Jason S. Price. 2006. "E-journal Interface Can Influence Usage Statistics: Implications for Libraries, Publishers, and Project COUNTER." *Journal of the American Society for Information Science and Technology* 57 no. 9: 1243–1248. doi:10.1002/asi.20405.

Dean, Caroline E., and Karin de Jager. 2009. "Statistics for Electronic Resources." *South African Journal of Library & Information Science* 75 no. 1: 76–85.

Fleming-May, Rachel A., and Jill E. Grogg. 2010. "Chapter 1: Assessing Use and Usage." *Library Technology Reports* 46, no. 6: 5–10. http://alatechsource.metapress.com/content/l73175817048j87q/fulltext.pdf.

GALILEO (GeorgiA LIbrary LEarning Online). 2011. "GALILEO Usage Statistics." Board of Regents of the University System of Georgia. http://about.galileo.usg.edu/statistics/.

Henle, Alea. 2007. "Electronic Resources (ER) Librarians, Usage Data, and a Changing World." *Collection Management* 32 no. 3/4: 277–288. doi:10.1300/J105v32n03_03.

Kyrillidou, Martha, and Les Bland. 2009. "Research Library Trends Tables and Graphs." *ARL Statistics 2007–2008*. www.arl.org/bm~doc/arlstat08.pdf.

Levine-Clark, Michael. 2006. "Electronic Book Usage: A Survey at the University of Denver." *Portal: Libraries and the Academy* 6, no. 3: 285–299.

Nagra, Kanu A. 2009. "The Evaluation of Use of Electronic Resources and Services in Academic Libraries: A Study of E-metrics and Related Methods for Measurement and Assessment." *Journal of the Library Administration & Management Section* 5, no. 3: 28–41. www.nyla.org/content/user_10/JLAMS_09_10V6N1.pdf.

NISO (National Information Standards Organization). 2005. "NISO Initiative to Standardize Online Usage Statistics Harvesting." National Information Standards Organization. www.niso.org/workrooms/sushi/info/SushiPRII.html.

———. 2011. "Standardized Usage Statistics Harvesting Initiative (SUSHI)." National Information Standards Organization. www.niso.org/workrooms/sushi/#about.

PRWeb. 2011. "Wolper Delivers PaperStats Technology to WOLPERweb Customers." PRWeb.com. December 1. www.prweb.com/releases/prweb2011/12/prweb9004705.htm.

Sprague, Nancy, and Ben Hunter. 2008. "Assessing E-books: Taking a Closer Look at E-book Statistics." *Library Collections, Acquisitions, & Technical Services* 32, no. 3/4: 150–157. doi:10.1016/j.lcats.2008.12.005.

Twain, Mark. 2006. *Chapters from My Autobiography*. Project Gutenberg. www.gutenberg. org/files/19987/19987-h/19987-h.htm. Previously published as "Chapters from My Autobiography. --XX." *North American Review*, no. 618 (1907): 465–474.

Chapter Seven

Staffing Changes to Facilitate the Shift to Electronic Resources

Denise Pan

How has the shift from print to electronic resources changed work in technical services? Do libraries have the human resources needed to cope with new challenges? What new skills are needed? Many libraries struggle to manage workloads with sufficient numbers and levels. Ideally, they can hire new staff members with the experience to make an immediate impact on the organization. In reality, it is often difficult to find knowledgeable candidates, or the library lacks the ability to create or replace positions. To further exacerbate the situation, the constantly evolving digital landscape makes it difficult to establish processes and procedures. This chapter explores the current environment as a catalyst for work flow and workload changes, while identifying some of the skills librarians need to manage online materials, and shares strategies for creating effective teams and implementing efficient work flow.

In many respects, these organizational management approaches could apply to all librarians, and possibly to other industries. However, working with electronic resources, librarians no longer have the luxury of continuing with the status quo and pretending that these challenges do not exist. To fulfill their responsibility of making electronic resources accessible and discoverable, they must adapt the way in which they perform their job functions and interact with others. Formal training may not exist or be possible; instead, in the new reality, "the focus is on employees 'learning-by-doing' with one another through problem solving and ideation for formulating new knowledge" (Pan and Howard, 2010: 497). Potentially, electronic resources librarians could be the trailblazers for the profession, leading the way forward in the new economy.

MEETING THE NEEDS OF A DYNAMIC ELECTRONIC ENVIRONMENT

The current environment is a stimulant for change. In these turbulent times, librarians experience challenges in all sizes and shapes. A poor economy produces tight budgets for library materials and operations and limits an organization's ability to add or replace staff. In addition, new technological developments create new formats, which add more complexity to purchasing and managing electronic resources. The acquisition-to-access phases of the electronic resources life cycle (see figure 1.2 in chapter 1) can require months to complete. How is the librarian able to cope within this context? What skills are needed?

The highly interconnected and complicated nature of online resources requires librarians to have a variety of qualities (see the Summary of Needed Skills sidebar). Conger (2004) suggests that the librarian must be able "to meet the many changes of the electronic environment with adroitness and flexibility and a weather eye toward a future filled with more change" (p. 46). Henle (2007) also describes the importance of flexibility, "since change is a given in the digital arena, librarians must be able to work with a constantly moving target" (p. 282). Other related and beneficial personality traits include the ability to deal with unintended consequences and the patience to see lengthy projects to the end.

Working with electronic resources, a single project or activity can incorporate a barrage of smaller details that may have unexpected results. For example, changes to the access and discovery of online materials could impact public services colleagues and patrons in unappreciated ways. The librarian walks a fine line between focusing on micro and macro issues because decisions made along the way often have unanticipated results on the bigger picture down the road. Dealing with an environment perpetually in motion, there are often more exceptions to established practices. Therefore, the librarian frequently needs to develop new solutions to complex issues (Pan and Lugg, 2010).

It goes without saying—the librarian should be "good with computers." Ability to learn quickly while using software applications and electronic tools is essential. Furthermore, skills with organizing, managing, and analyzing spreadsheets are immensely valuable. This expertise is particularly useful with title lists and usage data (Henle, 2007).

Librarians constantly communicate with colleagues (internally) as well as with vendors and publishers (externally). They cannot work in isolation. To achieve intended outcomes, they must work with others to understand and examine local needs and situations (Henle, 2007). In addition, the librarian may need to convey highly complicated and ambiguous information "to listeners who understand technology at widely varied levels. More often

SUMMARY OF NEEDED SKILLS

- Flexibility
- Multitasking
- Problem solving
- Technological capabilities
- Communication and collaboration
- Negotiation

than not, the members of this latter group are decision-makers/funding authorities and may be skeptical" (Downes and Rao, 2007: 11).

Depending on the library's organizational structure, the librarian may also need negotiation skills. In particular, if the position includes acquisitions responsibilities, license agreements and purchase details will be discussed with vendors and publishers. Developing an influential and persuasive style takes time and experience. Most librarians receive little or no formal training in this area and have learned on the job (Pomerantz, 2010).

Essentially, these skills can be grouped into two categories: internal and external. With flexibility, multitasking, problem solving, and technological capabilities, the electronic resources librarian can be self-reliant and self-sufficient. These traits are vital when established practices are practically nonexistent. However, the scope of managing electronic resources is too broad for one person. The ability to communicate, collaborate, and negotiate with others further expands the individual's capacity. Together, the librarian and colleagues are more apt to learn, adapt, and improve internal library processes to meet existing and future challenges.

BEING AN ORGANIZATIONAL LEADER

It is very likely that not all library colleagues are going to recognize that the evolving electronic environment requires the existing organization to modify daily routines. Conger (2004) argues: "When library professionals cease to learn, we freeze ourselves into skill sets and modes of thinking that were once relevant but do not follow the spiral of new realities" (p. 26). Regardless of rank or decision-making authority, all employees can demonstrate leadership. Both new and existing members of an organization have unique perspectives that can be leveraged to be convincing motivators of change. Recent hires can ask naive questions that may be controversial for others. Established employees already know the politics and the strengths and weaknesses of colleagues. All of these perspectives are valuable and can be leveraged to develop a collaborative organization that overcomes the challenges of online materials. This section describes some tactics for developing a learning culture when librarians need to implement strategies to influence supervisors, manage employees, and coach colleagues.

Managing Up: Managing Interactions and Information Flow with Superiors

Regardless of the library's hierarchical organizational structure, it is likely that the electronic resources librarian will report to a manager, supervisor, or administrator. Since this individual has ultimate decision-making authority, the librarian is at a power disadvantage. Darling and Cluff (1987) assert that "strategies used by subordinates to influence their administrators" or efforts to "managing up" can help increase influence of employees and attain compliance by supervisors (p. 350).

For example, if a proposal or plan requires management approval, the librarian should begin by asking to schedule an appointment to discuss the proposal with his or her manager. This more formal approach may be appropriate when requesting equipment, staffing, or outsourced services that require additional resources; for example, the electronic resources librarian may be managing usage statistics manually and believes that improved efficiencies and assessment capabilities could be achieved by subscribing to an e-resource assessment service. The meeting to propose the subscription can be requested in person or via e-mail but should clearly and concisely describe the reasons for the meeting.

GENERAL TIPS FOR PRESENTING A CONVINCING PROPOSAL

- Be on time
- Arrive prepared with talking points and handouts
- Know your audience by avoiding unfamiliar jargon or technical terms, and providing appropriate levels of detail
- Respond positively to questions and misconceptions
- Respect time limitations

After the meeting, send a follow-up e-mail thanking the supervisor for the time and summarize any agreements, next steps, or action items; include any due dates or deadlines. Should efforts fail and the proposal is rejected, a thank-you e-mail conveys respect, and if appropriate, mentions the possibility of revisiting the topic at a later date (Darling and Cluff, 1987).

In addition, it is useful to identify the supervisor's social style or interpersonal behaviors and modify one's own actions to exercise influence on theirs. The intention, however, is not to imitate or manipulate the manager. Rather, the goal of managing up is for the employee to "function effectively and comfortably within an area of commonality with his or her administrator . . . [and] when styles become complementary when strengths and weaknesses become compensatory" (Darling and Cluff, 1987: 355). To do so, subordinates must understand themselves as well as others.

Darling and Cluff (1987) offer practical suggestions for identifying, understanding, and accommodating diverse social styles (see tables 7.1 and 7.2). They

Table 7.1. Summary of Basic Social Styles

Social Style	Strengths	Weaknesses	Negative Reactions
Amiable	• Cooperative • Loyal • Supportive • Diplomatic	• Conforming • Permissive	• Acquiescing • Attacking • Avoiding • Autocratic
Analytical	• Logical • Thorough • Serious • Systematic	• Exacting • Inflexible	• Avoiding • Autocratic • Acquiescing • Attacking
Driver	• Independent • Candid • Decisive • Pragmatic	• Dominating • Insensitive	• Autocratic • Avoiding • Attacking • Acquiescing
Expressive	• Imaginative • Friendly • Enthusiastic • Outgoing	• Undisciplined • Unrealistic	• Attacking • Acquiescing • Autocratic • Avoiding

Source: Adapted from Darling and Cluff, 1987, Figures 2 and 3: 352.

identify four basic social styles—amiable, analytical, driver, and expressive—based on the work of Bolton and Bolton (1984). It is important for librarians or other professionals working with electronic resources to master these concepts. Effective communications skills are essential when conveying the intricacies of the legal aspects of contracts and the technical aspects of managing an electronic resources collection with superiors.

Supervising Employees

The manager, supervisor, or administrator has authority and directs the actions of subordinates. Making unilateral command decisions may be necessary during emergencies and time-sensitive situations. However these resolutions "have a high risk of failure" because "a crucial piece of information not known at the time of decision often proves fatal to implementation" (Conger, 2004: 26). The unintended consequences and complexity of the online environment elevates the importance of sharing knowledge at the point of need.

One way to avoid making uninformed resolutions is to develop a culture of learning and sharing through collaborative evidence-based information practices. This organizational management strategy shifts decision making from top-down by employers to bottom-up by employees (Pan and Howard, 2009). When roles and responsibilities are clearly defined, managers can practice centralized administration and distributed decision making. Each team member leads his or her area of specialization, but the work flow is managed collectively. The whole procedure is not considered complete until everyone has completed his or her portion of the process (Pan and Lugg, 2010).

To create a learning organization, face-to-face meetings should be scheduled on a routine and an ad hoc basis. Group discussions are most effective if agendas are collaboratively created and supplementary information is made available in advance. The most creative solutions and best decisions can surface when dialogue is encouraged. Maureen Sullivan (2004) defines the practice of dialogue as "meaningful conversation that seeks understanding at a deeper level and calls for balanced participation to enable the different voices to be heard" (pp. 225–226). Quickly afterward, meeting minutes should be posted and include action items, assignments, and time lines to achieve shared outcomes. This is particularly useful for short memories or when attendance is not possible.

Librarians of all areas of specialization should be proponents of information literacy. According to the Association of College & Research Libraries (2000),

Table 7.2. Strategies for Modifying Own Style
and Responding to Other's Style

Social Style	Modifying Own Style (If you are . . .)	Responding to Other's Style (If your supervisor is . . .)
Amiable	• Demonstrate self-direction • Attempt to achieve tough goals • Communicate important points • Challenge others to do their best	• Speak softly and at moderate pace • Maintain eye contact • Encourage discussion and no-pressure decision making • Provide solutions to maximize benefits and minimize risks
Analytical	• Make an effort to make a decision, even if not all facts are available • Avoid letting careful analysis prevent others from progressing • Follow through with action items once decision has been made	• Speak in moderate tone and pace • Act and dress more formally • Present information systematically • Provide pros and cons, and alternative solutions • Encourage throughout decision-making process
Driven	• Try to listen to questions and concerns of others • Be aware and understanding of their feelings and values • Validate their perceptions	• Speak at a fast pace • Maintain direct eye contact • Provide key facts succinctly and in a logical order • Present most effective options, and the pros and cons of each • If appropriate, ask for decision or next steps
Expressive	• Restrain impulsiveness • Be aware of other's reactions to high energy and excessive verbal activity • Let others speak first	• Speak with energy and fast pace • Allow for social and off-topic conversation; try to discover their dreams • Expect to debate • Provide testimonials as supporting evidence • Describe big picture ideas first, and then provide details • Rephrase decisions

Source: Adapted from Darling and Cluff, 1987, Tables 1 and 2: 353–354.

information literacy "forms the basis for lifelong learning. . . . It enables learners to master content and extend their investigations, become more self-directed, and assume greater control over their own learning." Lifelong learning in the workplace encourages colleagues to learn from one another as well as participate in professional development activities. Useful information can be obtained by subscribing to e-mail lists such as SERIALST (Serials in Libraries Discussion Forum) and ERIL-L (Electronic Resources in Libraries). Budget permitting, employees can attend conferences and participate in online webinars. Some recommended conferences include Electronic Resources & Libraries (www.electroniclibrarian.com), North American Serials Interest Group (www.nasig.org/conference_registration.cfm), and the Charleston Conference (www.katina.info/conference/). Practical webinars are available from ALCTS (Association for Library Collections and Technical Services). Furthermore, the workplace culture must be a safe place to make mistakes. Otherwise, individuals are discouraged from learning while doing. Colleagues should support and encourage initiative but also practice understanding, patience, and forgiveness when efforts fall short.

The perpetually shifting nature of electronic resources produces an environment where the status is always changing. Today the journal is accessible and discoverable, but tomorrow the URL or platform may change, making the full-text article no longer available. Staff members must troubleshoot the problems. However, they may be able to avoid some of these issues by identify-

---

EFFECTIVE COACHING SKILLS CHECKLIST

- ☐ Actively listen
- ☐ Demonstrate respect and acceptance
- ☐ Offer help and assistance
- ☐ Demonstrate care and concern
- ☐ Convey empathy
- ☐ Value others
- ☐ Allow time to vent feelings
- ☐ Encourage open and direct communication
- ☐ Clarify the situation
- ☐ Identify options
- ☐ Plan solutions
- ☐ Outline consequences
- ☐ Observe behavior and nonverbal cues
- ☐ Ask effective questions
- ☐ Paraphrase
- ☐ Offer and receive feedback

Source: Adapted from Stueart and Sullivan, 2010: 60.

ing important announcements from vendors, passing the details to the appropriate personnel, and implementing necessary changes. Having routine meetings and an intranet to share information encourages teams to be proactive instead of reactive. The staff members or other subordinates within an electronic resources department will be faced with many challenges in dealing with new technologies, legal concepts, and volume of workload. It is important for a manager in this type of department to encourage communication and collaboration that potentially can reduce stress or workload. While this can be said of all professions, it is especially important in the realm of electronic resources.

Coaching Colleagues

Setting up and maintaining access to online materials can be problematic for a variety of reasons. Often it "takes a village" because each person has a different perspective that contributes to identifying and creating solutions. Working collaboratively in groups, the electronic resources librarian needs to find productive ways to interact with colleagues. According to John Whitmore (2002), "Coaching is unlocking a person's potential to maximize their own performance. It is helping them to learn rather than teaching them" (p. 8). Ruth Metz (2010) describes coaching as "the purposeful and skillful effort by one individual to help another achieve specific performance goals" (p. 34). Moreover, coaching is a process of encouraging, enabling, and empowering an individual to assess the situation, identify goals, and develop a plan to achieve aspirations.

Coaching can be an effective strategy for improving an organization's effectiveness and ability to adapt to changes. Libraries that practice coaching can benefit from improved clarification, prioritization, leadership, performance, and problem-solving abilities (Metz, 2010). From a single conversation or multiple ongoing discussions, the workplace coaching experience encourages individuals "to analyze their strengths and weaknesses and to challenge their ways of thinking and doing in order to achieve higher levels of performance" (Stueart and Sullivan, 2010: 59).

Coaching is applicable in all workplace interactions: supervisor-staff; employee-boss; and colleague-colleague. Successful coaching relationships are based on trust. When "evoking excellence in others," James Flaherty (1999) believes that "roles may provide the circumstances, but only the relationship can provide the foundation" (p. 45). Both people must have a shared commitment and mutual trust, respect, and freedom of expression. Effective coaches guide, provide support, encourage development, and challenge thinking; they do not command, instruct, punish, or dictate. To be successful, coaching requires a variety of skills. Stueart and Sullivan (2010) offer a checklist for aspiring coaches to identify current and developing areas of competencies (see sidebar).

In the workplace, when there are no formal hierarchical relationships, peer coaching can be an effective strategy. Lacking a clear and established leader, the group becomes the decision maker. Practicing peer coaching enables the individuals to come together and implement effective teamwork, collaboration, and decision making. John Lubans Jr. (2010) identifies six peer coaching skills, "collective listening, time management, delegation of responsibility, being prepared, being proactive, [and] communication—talking and giving feedback" (p. 35).

While coaching may be used in all professions, it is a vitally important skill for individuals managing an electronic resources department. This is particularly useful when the electronic resources work flow and troubleshooting are distributed among a team of people. The selection-to-access continuum may take months to complete, and access issues are typically unplanned. Each member of the team needs to recognize his or her roles, responsibilities, and relationships to colleagues. When tasks are completed, others should be informed so they can begin their assignment. Electronic resources is a very dynamic field that is changing all the time and thus a supervisor in this type of department will be in a constant state of teaching new skill sets for new resources and interfaces.

CREATING AND MAINTAINING TEAMS

The roles and responsibilities of librarians managing electronic resources are still in transition. Libraries have been restructuring to adapt to the emphasis on digital for over a decade. Despite this, surprisingly there is no standard organizational chart or job description for managing online resources (Pomerantz, 2010). When considering staffing structure, it is often an "either or" proposition. Should skills, knowledge, and authority be centralized with one person or decentralized among many? Does the size of library budgets and online collections impact the volume of work and size of workforce?

Centralization enables specialization and development of expertise but may limit capacity or ability to manage increasing quantity. The person may have tacit knowledge that is difficult to share with others. Pomerantz (2010) also explains that "reliance on individual expertise creates the risk that the system could break down if one person is unavailable or leaves the institution" (p. 42). Distribution of responsibility requires breaking tasks into manageable components, creating consistent procedures, and practicing clear communication. While this strategy helps with managing scale, it may be difficult to implement in the short term and may hinder big picture awareness in the long term (Pan and Lugg, 2010).

With the dynamic nature of electronic resource management, technical services departments need to reorganize staff with the right attitude and aptitude (see the Summary of Needed Skills sidebar, earlier in this chapter). Each library has its own unique local situation and existing employees. To facilitate the reorganization and work flow redesign, all stakeholders should be invited to contribute to the process. Participation can lead to consensus when staff input is requested, all views are considered, and group cooperation is celebrated (Stueart and Sullivan, 2010). Appreciative inquiry and backcasting are two strategic approaches for creating and maintaining collaborative teams.

Appreciative Inquiry (AI)

Strategic planning, restructuring, redesigning work, and project management are typical library organizational development efforts that benefit from AI. Instead of focusing on problems and negative issues, AI looks toward what has worked in the past and the best possibilities for the future. It encourages individuals to become active participants in change by contributing their ideas and knowledge.

A supervisor conducting an "Appreciative Inquiry Interview" or sharing stories is an effective way to implement the model. Begin by asking an individual or group of stakeholders questions about their experiences, accomplishments, and ideas. For example:

- When did you feel most engaged in your work?
- What is your greatest contribution?
- What are the library's best attributes?
- What aspirations do you have for the library?

APPRECIATIVE INQUIRY PROCESS

The AI process is based on a 4-D cycle with four stages:

1. Discovery: Appreciate "what is" or past examples of success.

2. Dream: Imagine "what might be" or envision the possibilities.

3. Design: Determine "what should be" or develop the plan.

4. Destiny: Create "what will be" or achieve the goals.

- What are the sources of pride in your work?
- Who in the library exemplifies leadership? What did that person do? How did that impact you?
- When do you feel creative?
- What was your best experience at work? What enabled this to occur?

AI develops collaboration because it engages participants through conversation. Verbalizing the possibilities shows appreciation of effort and commitment. This encouragement motivates staff to continue learning. The contribution of the individual, within the growth of the organization, is emphasized throughout the process (Sullivan, 2004).

Electronic resources librarians should consider using AI when introducing new and controversial ideas. If staff is comfortable with existing work flow and systems, switching to a service or launching new software may be demoralizing. For instance, a cataloger may be responsible for copy cataloging bibliographic records for electronic journals. If the library decided to subscribe to an outsource MARC record service, the cataloger's responsibility will be impacted. Implementing AI is a way to give the cataloger an opportunity to participate in discussion and identify future goals.

Backcasting

A supervisor may choose to use backcasting in addition to AI. Similar to AI, the concept of backcasting is centered on the inquiry process and asking relevant and thought-provoking questions. Derived from sustainable development research, this strategic approach asks participants to envision a desirable future, and then move backward to plan the steps required to achieve the intended outcome. Backcasting is a relevant planning methodology, and "it is a complement to forecasting, and is particularly relevant when the problems we are dealing with

SEVEN STEPS TO IMPLEMENT BACKCASTING

1. Identify and invite all stakeholders to participate.

2. Define purpose or goals of meeting.

3. Explain principles of backcasting.

4. Brainstorm the ideal future.

5. Ask "what needs to happen today to achieve our vision?"

6. Document discussion.

7. Identify next steps.

are complex, and when today's trends are part of the problem" (Holmberg and Karl-Henrik, 2000: 305).

In the context of a library and managing electronic resources, backcasting can be a useful exercise when

- there are concerns that important process/procedures are not incorporated into existing work flow and may be forgotten;
- a relatively newly formed team does not have intimate understanding of colleagues' responsibilities;
- potentially essential information is not being communicated to the appropriate person at time of need; and
- necessary information is not always readily and easily available or is stored in multiple personal and shared locations.

When implementing backcasting, the process encourages collaboration and communication. Brainstorming activities can be performed individually or in small groups. Using poster boards and colored pens to draw pictures can help inspire creativity. Throughout the experience, ask questions to identify and clarify the situation:

- What are the assumptions?
- What are the investments?
- What are the consequences?

Ideally, through discussion and dialogue the contributors will be able to identify the major objectives, set immediate and long-term priorities, identify measurements for success, and assign action items. Using strategies like these will allow the department to become a more cohesive whole and allow past issues or situations to be evaluated in a positive light.

When there are e-resources work flow issues, backcasting can offer a way to approach issues, find solutions, and avoid placing blame on individuals. Enabling off-campus access, as an example, may require numerous steps by several different people. If someone forgets his or her part, patrons cannot access online library materials from home. With a specific known outcome in mind, the team can use backcasting to develop best practices and procedures.

Training New and Existing Staff

Moving from print to electronic resources requires new skills. Some staff will naturally rise to the occasion, while most will require some encouragement and guidance. Regardless of whether employees are new or existing members of the organization, they need continuing education. Formal trainings are offered by library software/hardware service vendors and associations, such as the American Library Association, Association for Library Collections and Technical Services, and North American Serials Interest Group. These organizations provide conferences, workshops, webinars, and publications. Topics typically focus on best practices, trends, and standards. Supervisors should be aware of free professional development opportunities, budget for registration expenses (when possible), and encourage employee participation.

Local library practices call for in-house training. As baby boomer library employees consider retirement, responsibilities of existing staff will be redefined and these new duties may require retraining. Furthermore, electronic resources provide users with 24/7 access to library materials. Lapse in service because an employee is on vacation is unacceptable. Therefore, librarians working with electronic resources must be cross-trained to troubleshoot problems.

Experienced staff may be able to absorb procedures by observing and learning by doing. In contrast, new hires and reluctant learners may need more guidance. Demonstrating and documenting procedures is an effective way to teach new skills. Although this process initially time-consuming, the learner will benefit from multiple sessions of "job shadowing" or observing how the trainer completes his or her work. Job shadowing is a viable teaching strategy for both retraining and cross-training. Sitting side by side over multiple sessions, the teacher and student can transform explicit tasks into tacit knowledge. At a minimum, the job shadowing process consists of three sessions:

- First session: Trainer slowly models step-by-step process, and learner takes notes.
- Second session: Trainer repeats step-by-step process while learner reads and edits notes.
- Third session: Learner consults notes and repeats step-by-step process while trainer follows along.

Repeat the third session until trainer and learner are confident that the learner is able to repeat the procedures on his or her own.

The two essential ingredients for successful training are patience and encouragement. As employees are taught new skills, they may initially feel devalued and vulnerable. It is imperative that the supervisor/trainer dissuade these sentiments. Celebrate the successes regardless of size. Mistakes should be recognized as a learning opportunity. The significance of making an error is minimized. Over time, their confidence and experience will grow.

SUMMARY

The shift from print to electronic resources has dramatically changed work in technical services. Many libraries are struggling to meet new challenges with their existing human resources. Within the context of a changing online environment and unstable economy, electronic resources librarians must learn and adapt with colleagues to find solutions. They cannot afford to sit idly and complacently with established practices. With their unique skill set, they are well equipped to demonstrate how to learn on the job and become organizational leaders and models for the profession. Regardless of hierarchical relationship, there is a thoughtful way to work and create knowledge with others. When managing up, the electronic resources librarians should recognize and modify their own actions so they will be most receptive to the supervisor's social style. As a manager, the librarian can change workplace culture through collaborative evidence-based information practices and by promoting lifelong learning. Coaching coworkers can motivate individuals to achieve their own aspirations. Practicing appreciative inquiry and backcasting permits stakeholders to reorganize staff and maintain work flow. With these strategic approaches, the librarian has a toolbox of effective strategies to create and maintain collaborative and cohesive working teams.

REFERENCES

ACRL (Association of College & Research Libraries). 2000. "Information Literacy Competency Standards for Higher Education." Association of College & Research Libraries. www.ala.org/ala/mgrps/divs/acrl/standards/informationliteracycompetency.cfm.

Bolton, Robert, and Dorothy Grover Bolton. 1984. *Social Style Management Style.* New York: American Management Association.

Conger, Joan E. 2004. *Collaborative Electronic Resource Management.* Westport, CT: Libraries Unlimited.

Darling, John R., and E. Dale Cluff. 1987. "Social Styles and the Art of Managing Up." *Journal of Academic Librarianship* 12, no. 6 (January): 350–355.

Downes, Kathy A., and Pal V. Rao. 2007. "Preferred Political, Social, and Technological Characteristics of Electronic Resources (ER) Librarians." *Collection Management* 32, no. 1/2 (January): 3–14. Library, Information Science & Technology Abstracts, EBSCOhost.

Flaherty, James. 1999. *Coaching: Evoking Excellence in Others.* Boston: Butterworth-Heinemann.

Henle, Alea. 2007. "Electronic Resources (ER) Librarians, Usage Data, and a Changing World." *Collection Management* 32, no. 3/4 (July): 277–288.

Holmberg, John, and Robert, Karl-Henrik. 2000. "Backcasting from Non-overlapping Sustainability Principles—A Framework for Strategic Planning." *International Journal of Sustainable Development and World Ecology* 7, no. 4 (December): 291–308.

Lubans, John, Jr. 2010. "Peer Coaching in the Post-Departmental Library." *Library Leadership & Management* 24, no. 1 (Winter): 33–37.

Metz, Ruth. 2010. "Coaching in the Library." *American Libraries* 41, no. 3 (March): 34–37.

Pan, Denise, and Zaana Howard. 2009. "Reorganizing a Technical Services Division Using Collaborative Evidence Based Information Practice at Auraria Library." *Evidence Based Library and Information Practice* 4, no 4: 88–94.

———. 2010. "Distributing Leadership and Cultivating Dialogue with Collaborative EBIP." *Library Management* 31, no. 7: 494–504.

Pan, Denise, and Rick Lugg. 2010. "Scaling Organizational Capacity to Meet E-resources Needs: Centralize or Decentralize?" Paper presented at Electronic Resources & Libraries, Austin, TX, February 2.

Pomerantz, Sarah B. 2010. "The Role of the Acquisitions Librarian in Electronic Resources Management." *Journal of Electronic Resources Librarianship* 22, no. 1/2 (January): 40–48.

Stueart, Robert D., and Maureen Sullivan. 2010. *Developing Library Leaders: A How-To-Do-It Manual for Coaching, Team Building, and Mentoring Library Staff.* New York: Neal-Schuman.

Sullivan, Maureen. 2004. "The Promise of Appreciative Inquiry in Library Organizations." *Library Trends* 53, no. 1 (Summer): 218–229.

Whitmore, John. 2002. *Coaching for Performance: GROWing People, Performance and Purpose.* London: Nicholas Brealey.

Chapter Eight

Looking Ahead from Now to 2020

George Stachokas

L ibrarianship as a profession is closely linked to how our society stores, retrieves, and manipulates information. Computerization, the development of the Internet, and the emergence of new communication tools, especially mobile devices (Duderstadt, 2009), have changed how information is managed outside the library and will also have an impact within. Electronic resources are at the heart of these changes, and while it is not possible to predict the future many years from now, at least not with great accuracy, we can consider future developments during the next five to ten years that will impact the broad specialization of electronic resources management. To put it simply, what might happen between now and 2020?

HOW E-BOOKS MAY CHANGE LIBRARIES

Newly published e-books will outnumber printed books among new publications by 2020. The demise of the printed book has been predicted many times before and it would be foolish to argue that print books will disappear entirely, but it is increasingly accepted by most critical observers across the world that a tipping point has been reached with e-books (Bedord, 2009). Amazon now sells more e-books than paperbacks (Hardawar, 2011). Brick-and-mortar bookstores like Borders have closed their doors. Tablets such as the iPad and e-readers such as the Kindle and Nook are now widely available in developed countries and provide unprecedented convenience for reading digital content. Electronic textbooks are starting to take off. Even small university presses are arguably scrambling to make their content available online through Project Muse/UPCC, JSTOR, and other online platforms. The first e-book was produced in 1971 by Project Gutenberg, and a combination of generational change, improvements in technology, and consumer convenience will make the electronic format the preferred format for books by 2020.

Problems of Access

While e-books will be the preferred format, libraries in the developing world, remote areas, and underprivileged areas in the developed world are not likely to be able to make the transition from print to electronic very easily. The impact of technological change, declining public sector support, and the economic crisis have already forced some libraries to close, and the digital divide may grow wider for some communities by 2020 (Bélanger and Carter, 2009). While some vendors and not-for-profit entities have made electronic content available to underfunded libraries at little or no cost and there are many freely available electronic resources to choose from, libraries that cannot afford to make the transition to the electronic format will increasingly find it difficult to serve their users with a shrinking pool of print publications (Zia et al., 2009).

Overcoming these gaps will be difficult, and Jeffrey James (2008) has argued that the problem will be far more difficult to overcome than has been commonly accepted to date. It is not necessary to address a single problem such as a skills deficit, digital infrastructure, or income, but all of these problems must be addressed simultaneously (James, 2008).

Popular works are likely to continue to be available in print, if only for marketing purposes, but most new government information is already available to libraries only in electronic format, and most new works in the humanities, sciences, and professions will increasingly be readily available only in electronic format. It is possible that surviving chain bookstores will stock only a few copies of print titles for browsing and display while users will be able to download and print copies on demand with various fees for different types of binding, illustrations, and other options. Libraries may also choose to purchase or make facilities available for print on demand with or without additional fees charged to the individual user as another option to access books. Print-on-demand books will essentially be e-books that can be printed out in fancy ways, however, and most busy users will prefer to download and read their e-book on their e-reader or mobile device. Just as personal computers have improved over time, we can expect tools for reading e-books to improve as well.

Electronic Resources Become the Primary Collection/Service of Libraries

The book has been fundamental to the development of the profession of librarianship. What does it mean when the book and other physical media are no longer the most important elements in the library's collection? Does the library continue to exist? Do we need librarians? Many nonlibrarians already ask these questions, and an increasing number say no. They think that they do not need librarians and they do not need libraries. To some extent the physical library has already been replaced by the Internet—the cloud, a vast unseen network of servers provided by publishers and other content providers scattered all over the world. So, strictly speaking, we no longer need the library of the nineteenth century or the twentieth century, but we do need to remind our users, and in some cases ourselves, that we all need the library of the twenty-first century, or at least the library of 2020.

The library of 2020 will feature a collection built primarily around electronic resources (Breeding, 2011), from both external and internal sources. Academic and some public libraries will continue to shrink their print collections as the relative cost of acquiring and providing access to print grows, usage of print declines, and more desirable uses of space are considered. Apart from law libraries, which seem to be unusually conservative regarding print, special libraries, especially medical libraries, will deaccession print as fast they can so that the newly built medical library in 2020 will closely resemble a comfortable Internet café or quite possibly be a multipurpose lounge with library personnel housed in adjoining or separate office space. For special libraries, library as place will be replaced with library as any place. This is already true to some extent, but special libraries will make no bones about deemphasizing the importance of space and location in providing information services.

Library Closures and Consolidation

Libraries that survive the economic crisis, budget cuts, technological change, and an increasingly skeptical user population will need to calculate how best to provide and market information services to their unique clientele (Mittrowann, 2009). Unfortunately, in some cases, the demand from those who provide financial support will simply be for some libraries to close. Branch public libraries will continue to close as electronic resources are accessible anywhere, and it is easier for state libraries and other large entities such as consortia to negotiate complex licenses, provide technology support, and train users. Departmental and branch libraries will also close on academic campuses, with libraries consolidating scarce resources and remaining personnel. This has already started with Cornell University's recent decision to replace physical departmental libraries with digital libraries as only one example (Koennecke and Kara, 2011). For most colleges and universities, while the possibilities and sustainability of library as place have yet to be fully explored (Jankowska and Marcum, 2010), the fact that the physical library will be one place on campus seems to be rather certain.

ORGANIZATIONAL CHANGE IN LIBRARIES

How will the primacy of electronic resources impact the individual library in terms of organizational structure? While some very small libraries will continue to exist, it is an interesting question as to what happens to larger academic, public, and some special libraries. Technical services based on 1970s-era automation will continue to consolidate and shrink over time. Some staff, including some librarians, will be retrained and repurposed, or their actual work will change even if their job titles lag behind in some cases. Catalogers will be increasingly replaced by metadata specialists (Lopatin, 2010). Metadata specialists will be expected to have greater knowledge, adaptability, and more general knowledge than catalogers who previously worked with MARC records. Metadata specialists will also more often work as part of larger complex units with professionals in other areas of specialization than as members of units that specialize only in cataloging or metadata. The ease of online ordering as well as the cessation of tasks such as binding, sorting packages, not to mention shifting physical materials around, will make it unnecessary to hire large numbers of staff who specialize in ordering and processing physical materials, making traditional acquisitions work less relevant to libraries.

Public Services

Reference and bibliographic instruction units will also need to adapt to ensure that their work continues to be relevant and supported by users and funding agencies. Improvements in search and discovery tools and the shift toward electronic resources reduce the need for a reference desk attendant who presides over a physical reference collection. Anne Grodzins Lipow (2003), who also wrote about the hypothetical library of 2020, has argued that well-trained paraprofessional staff can provide direct customer service while referring more complex questions to professional staff who make themselves available by appointment or other means. Who needs to thumb through paper almanacs, dictionaries, gazetteers, or encyclopedias anymore? Online library guides and tutorials, some provided by publishers or vendors, often teach users how to access information that is already increasingly intuitive to use with better-designed interfaces and complex algorithms, search suggestions, and other features that can help even the laziest user find relevant information. Does this mean that information literacy is irrelevant? No. Does it mean that libraries should fire all of their reference librarians? Absolutely and categorically, the answer is no. What it does mean is that reference must adapt to new user needs and new opportunities for librarians.

First and foremost, reference librarians need to be available at the point of need, particularly online need (Trump, Tuttle, and Dugan, 2001). Many librarians already do communicate via e-mail, online chat, or other online means, and this trend is likely to continue. The best opportunities for general reference are most likely to be available at public libraries while academic libraries will continue to hire subject specialists. Reference subject specialists will require greater specialized training in subject disciplines and will bring added value to the library and users by tracking trends in research and teaching, assisting students with using (not just finding) appropriate information, and providing more pedagogical assistance to instructors within and outside the classroom. Distance education will also put a greater emphasis on the library, as students without direct access to peers or easy access to instructors will turn to helpful librarians for additional assistance in navigating through complex coursework (Brahme and Walters, 2010).

Circulation or access services will continue to take primary responsibility for managing the library as place and staffing a public service desk of some type. As the print collection shrinks, staff dedicated to managing book stacks will be reduced in number, but other tasks have already and will continue to demand attention, such as providing assistance with the use of computers, printers, and other technology, answering basic questions about services, assisting disabled users, and providing general onsite customer service. Some staff in these areas may also provide assistance with electronic reserves and course management software to busy instructors, but it is important to note that many academic libraries have already shifted toward a self-service model for handling e-reserve functions (Goodson and Frederiksen, 2011).

Special Collections and Archives

Special collections and archival units will increasingly focus on digital information or digital resources. To some extent there is an artificial divide between the "electronic" and the "digital" resource, with the former being externally created and the latter being internally created. Nonetheless, it is to be expected that a distinction will continue between electronic and digital resources, with the latter falling under the umbrella of special collections in most libraries. Of course, there is likely to be some collaboration between electronic resources and digital resources personnel in managing metadata standards, library webpages, and search and discovery tools. As institutions continue to create new digital records to replace print records, librarians also have an opportunity to take pride of place as managers of those records (Case, 2008), although competition from other professional groups will be very strong. Nonetheless, it can be argued that librarians with archival training and other specialized skill sets would make excellent stewards of the public record.

Electronic Resources and Technical Services

Electronic resources as a department is likely to grow, as most libraries will decide to consolidate most licensing, acquisitions, metadata, assessment, and technology support functions in one department or division depending on the library's size. Given the dependence on library vendors and the consolidated administration of most electronic resource management tools, the integration of functions within a single administrative unit will be more efficient and less confusing than spreading these functions out among multiple departments (Stachokas, 2009). Expect new professional and paraprofessional positions that collect and interpret data for assessment and calculation of ROI (return on investment), building initially on the exploitation of COUNTER-compliant usage statistics, impact factors, and other metrics, but expanding into collecting data about user behavior and preferences, hopefully anonymous user data. Licensing and copyright functions will be consolidated, and one or more librarians will specialize in licensing, collection development for electronic resources, and the assessment of new technologies and services. The assessment process will likely require input from librarians in multiple departments or areas of specialization as the library attempts to make a strategic or holistic assessment of service. One example would be the Progressive Alignment Model for distance education proposed by Larry Nash White (2010). Librarians from larger academic and public libraries may hire new professionals who specialize in assessing technology, tracking trends, and recommending new strategies for development. Technology support and outreach, teaching users about technology, platforms, or devices, will likely continue even as technology becomes more accessible.

The wide range of tools and techniques and the exploding number of information sources will keep librarians busy even as technology becomes easier and easier to use without mediation. Above all, electronic resources specialists will become plural while remaining integrated administratively: specialists in licensing will have more legal training, especially in copyright law; specialists in assessment will have more training in statistics, among other things; specialists in technology support will have more training in IT and most likely collaborate or overlap with library systems or IT units. Another overlapping role between electronic resource management specialists, IT, and reference will be in collecting data about user behavior and using increasingly precise information to customize locally provided services.

Library systems and IT departments developed in the 1970s, as libraries invested in integrated library systems (ILSs) in order to use computers to manage acquisitions, cataloging, and circulation functions. This early phase of library automation was focused on using technology to manage print collections. A library collection based on electronic resources will continue to be supported by library IT personnel, at least at medium or larger libraries, but software as service will change how local servers are used. Expect library IT personnel to continue to work with growing institutional repositories and local digital archives, provide more direct technology support and customer service to users, and work closely or be administratively combined with electronic resource management personnel. Libraries, especially academic libraries at large institutions, will continue to invest in their own IT and hire specialists to manage technology even as librarians themselves acquire new IT skills.

Who Works for the Library?

The definition of who works for the library will become more fluid in various ways. Expect more short-term service contracts in which vendors provide additional assistance online or in person as libraries deploy new tools and technologies. Consortia may pool resources to hire and share specialized personnel, especially for print repositories, special climate-controlled facilities for special collections, rare books, and artifacts. Distance education librarians may not need to work physically at the library any more than distance education instructors or students must be based on campus.

CHALLENGES AND OPPORTUNITIES

Librarians face a number of challenges in providing a robust portfolio of electronic resources to their users. Using the word "collection" is inherently problematic given the virtual context of electronic resources, and "access" might be a better word, but the word "portfolio" is somewhat more descriptive, as it suggests the body of information that the library manages regardless of provenance. The rising costs of electronic resources, especially full-text databases and serials (King and Alvarado-Albertorio, 2008), is a terrible problem for cash-strapped libraries, while e-book business models have yet to take form. Librarians will need to ensure that vendors remain committed to resource sharing and scholarly sharing in order to guarantee that society's information needs are met.

Role of Consortia

Consortia will continue in importance and take on additional relevance by helping to set advantageous terms with vendors, by providing training to members, and through professional advocacy. Consortia may even take a role in helping to set standards and templates for best practices. Consortia have developed worldwide, particularly in China (Dong and Zou, 2009), India, and the Middle East during the past ten years (Moghaddam and Talawar, 2009). Consolidation of vendors is a threat, and given the monopolistic nature of the information market, libraries may need to work with partners outside the profession to keep costs down. If prices for electronic resources continue to rise at unsustainable levels, some kind of regulation is not inconceivable. Even as libraries are forced to cancel subscriptions due to budget cuts, many vendors attempt to retain their current revenue streams for "big deal" packages (Cryer and Grigg, 2011).

Consortia that do not help libraries to save money or provide services primarily based on yesterday's technology (e.g., the ILS) will cease to exist as functional organizations. This has already happened to a considerable extent, but consortia that do not save money for their members will lose their rationale for existence. A recent survey conducted by Katherine Perry (2009) has shown that the greatest focuses on consortia in 2009 were renegotiating licenses for electronic resources and budget management. Nonetheless, consortia will also find new opportunities. Consortia among libraries and higher education institutions in developing countries can also serve as a way to consolidate scarce resources and provide services such as distance education (Beaudoin, 2009). A challenge for consortia, at least in North America, has been the tendency among vendors to punish libraries that cancel resources or try to customize or alter "big deal" packages.

Open Access

The open access movement will not replace for-profit vendors, but it will help to ensure wider access to information and play at least a small role in keeping overall costs down. Electronic resources made freely available to users will be selected and tracked by libraries as appropriate for their unique user populations. It is difficult to predict success in 2020, but Barbara McFadden Allen (2008) has argued that librarians need to engage teaching faculty, cultivate administrators, and generally take a leading role in the development of institutional repositories. Public libraries, as a separate but related process, might also consider how they can provide digital repositories for information important to the local communities that they serve, such as the digitization of genealogical and community records, memorabilia, and other documentation that will be relevant to future students of cultural and social history.

145

From Collection Development to Information as Service

Libraries already provide access to a wide range of electronic resources from e-books to full-text databases, some of which are freely available and others are leased or purchased from various sources by a wide range of business models. Complexity is expected to continue, with libraries employing a mixture of purchasing, leasing, pay-per-view, patron-driven acquisition, and shared collections in order to maximize the amount of information useful to users. While libraries will hold many resources in common (e.g., large full-text databases such as EBSCO's Academic Search Premier or ProQuest Research Library), one should expect greater customization when free electronic resources and locally published electronic content are included in the mix. Depending on cost-per-use and other metrics, libraries will likely select from a range of business models for electronic resources rather than settling on a single dominant model, at least up to 2020. What happens after that is more difficult to predict.

Providing access, especially to expensive content, will continue to be an important service of the library, but the value added by libraries will be the whole package of services related to information management for specific user populations, rather than providing access to collections per se. Many vendors already directly market content for sale to users, and some users continue to prefer almost random Google searching to exploring what the library has to offer. Libraries will face competition as information providers (Thomas, 2011), but it will be in the area of service, not just access, that libraries will continue to provide additional value to users. Directing users to the right information will be critical because information is more widely available from more sources than ever before (Walter, 2011). Specialists in electronic resource management will specialize in licensing or providing access to the most appropriate information at the lowest available cost in money and staff time, collect data and provide analysis for assessment, oversee metadata standards, and provide technology support. Public services specialists will promote and teach information literacy, assist users with reference, and provide general customer service.

REFERENCES

Allen, Barbara McFadden. 2008. "All Hype or Real Change: Has the Digital Revolution Changed Scholarly Communication?" *Journal of Library Administration* 48, no. 1: 59–68.

Beaudoin, Michael F. 2009. "Consortia—A Viable Model and Medium for Distance Education in Developing Countries?" *Open Learning* 24, no. 2: 113–126.

Bedord, Jean. 2009. "Ebooks Hit Critical Mass: Where Do Libraries Fit with Oprah?" *Online* 33, no. 3: 14–18.

Bélanger, France, and Lemuria Carter. 2009. "The Impact of the Digital Divide on E-government Use." *Communications of the ACM* 52, no. 4: 132–135.

Brahme, Maria, and Lauren Walters. 2010. "While Technology Poses as the Great Equalizer, Distance Still Rules the Experience." *Journal of Library Administration* 50, no. 5/6: 484–514.

Breeding, Marshall. 2011. "The Systems Librarian: Preparing for the Long-Term Digital Future of Libraries." *Computers in Libraries* 31, no. 1: 24–26.

Case, Mary M. 2008. "Partners in Knowledge Creation: An Expanded Role for Research Libraries in the Digital Future." *Journal of Library Administration* 48, no. 2: 141–156.

Cryer, Emma, and Karen S. Grigg. 2011. "Consortia and Journal Package Renewal: Evolving Trends in the 'Big Package Deal'?" *Journal of Electronic Resources in Medical Libraries* 8, no. 1: 22–34.

Dong, Elaine Xiaofen, and Tim Jiping Zou. 2009. "Library Consortia in China." *LIBRES: Library & Information Science Research Electronic Journal* 19, no. 1: 1–10.

Duderstadt, James J. 2009. "Possible Futures for the Research Library in the 21st Century." *Journal of Library Administration* 49, no. 3: 217–225.

Goodson, Kymberly Anne, and Linda Frederiksen. 2011. "E-reserves in Transition: Exploring New Possibilities in E-reserves Service Delivery." *Journal of Interlibrary Loan, Document Delivery & Electronic Reserves* 21, no. 1/2: 33–56.

Hardawar, Devindra. 2011. "A Milestone for E-books: Amazon Sells More Kindle Books Than Print." *MediaBeat*, May 19, 2011. http://venturebeat.com/2011/05/19/kindle -books-surpass-print/.

James, Jeffrey. 2008. "Re-estimating the Difficulty of Closing the Digital Divide." *Journal of the American Society for Information Science & Technology* 59, no. 12: 2024–2032.

Jankowska, Maria Anna, and James W. Marcum. 2010. "Sustainability Challenge for Academic Libraries: Planning for the Future." *College & Research Libraries* 71, no. 2: 160–170.

King, Donald W., and Frances M. Alvarado-Albertorio. 2008. "Pricing and Other Means of Charging for Scholarly Journals: A Literature Review and Commentary." *Learned Publishing* 21, no. 4: 248–272.

Koennecke, Jesse, and Bill Kara. 2011. "Going Virtual Is Not Magic: Converting Physical Libraries to Virtual Libraries." Presentation, Electronic Resources & Libraries, Austin, TX, March 1.

Lipow, Anne Grodzins. 2003. "The Future of Reference: Point-of-Need Reference Service: No Longer an Afterthought." *Reference Services Review* 31, no. 1: 31–35.

Lopatin, Laurie. 2010. "Metadata Practices in Academic and Non-academic Libraries for Digital Projects: A Survey." *Cataloging & Classification Quarterly* 48, no. 8: 716–742.

Mittrowann, Andreas. 2009. "Strategic, Digital, Human: The Library of the Future: A View on International Developments by a German Library Supplier." *Public Library Quarterly* 28, no. 3 (July): 193–203.

Moghaddam, Golnessa Galyani, and V. G. Talawar. 2009. "Library Consortia in Developing Countries: An Overview." *Program: Electronic Library & Information Systems* 43, no. 1: 94–104.

Perry, Katherine A. 2009. "Where Are Library Consortia Going? Results of a 2009 Survey." *Serials* 22, no. 2: 122–130.

Stachokas, George. 2009. "Electronic Resources and Mission Creep: Reorganizing the Library for the Twenty-First Century." *Journal of Electronic Resources Librarianship* 21, no. 3/4: 206–212

Thomas, Lisa Carlucci. 2011. "Libraries and the Future of Electronic Content Delivery." *American Libraries* 42, no. 7/8: 24–25.

Trump, Judith F., Ian P. Tuttle, and Robert E. Dugan. 2001. "Here, There, and Everywhere: Reference at the Point-of-Need." *Journal of Academic Librarianship* 27, no. 6: 464.

Walter, Scott. 2011. "'Distinctive Signifiers of Excellence': Library Services and the Future of the Academic Library" (Guest Editorial). *College & Research Libraries* 72, no. 1: 6–8.

White, Larry Nash. 2010. "Aligning Assessment to Organizational Performance in Distance Education Service Delivery." *Journal of Library Administration* 50, no. 7/8: 997–1016.

Zia, Tanveer, Yeslam Al-Saggaf, Zahidul Islam, Zheng Lihong, and John Weckert. 2009. "The Digital Divide in Asia." *Journal of Information Ethics* 18, no. 2: 50–76.

Historical and Current Copyright Law Excerpts

Editor's Note

All of the following content has been taken directly from the URLs cited in the References section at the end of the appendix. These government documents can be accessed via the Internet in their entirety but are included here as a quick reference for readers of this guide.

United States Constitution Section 8, Clause 8

To promote the Progress of Science and useful Arts, by securing for limited Times to Authors and Inventors the exclusive Right to their respective Writings and Discoveries. (U.S. House of Representatives, 2004)

Section 106 of Chapter 1 of Title 17

Subject to sections 107 through 122, the owner of copyright under this title has the exclusive rights to do and to authorize any of the following:

> (1) to reproduce the copyrighted work in copies or phonorecords;
>
> (2) to prepare derivative works based upon the copyrighted work;
>
> (3) to distribute copies or phonorecords of the copyrighted work to the public by sale or other transfer of ownership, or by rental, lease, or lending;

(4) in the case of literary, musical, dramatic, and choreographic works, panto-mimes, and motion pictures and other audiovisual works, to perform the copyrighted work publicly;

(5) in the case of literary, musical, dramatic, and choreographic works, panto-mimes, and pictorial, graphic, or sculptural works, including the individual images of a motion picture or other audiovisual work, to display the copy-righted work publicly; and

(6) in the case of sound recordings, to perform the copyrighted work publicly by means of a digital audio transmission. (U.S. Copyright Office, 2009)

Section 107 of Chapter 1 of Title 17

Limitations on exclusive rights: Fair use

Notwithstanding the provisions of sections 106 and 106A, the fair use of a copy-righted work, including such use by reproduction in copies or phonorecords or by any other means specified by that section, for purposes such as criticism, comment, news reporting, teaching (including multiple copies for classroom use), scholar-ship, or research, is not an infringement of copyright. In determining whether the use made of a work in any particular case is a fair use the factors to be considered shall include—

(1) the purpose and character of the use, including whether such use is of a commercial nature or is for nonprofit educational purposes;

(2) the nature of the copyrighted work;

(3) the amount and substantiality of the portion used in relation to the copy-righted work as a whole; and

(4) the effect of the use upon the potential market for or value of the copy-righted work.

The fact that a work is unpublished shall not itself bar a finding of fair use if such finding is made upon consideration of all the above factors.

Section 108 of Chapter 1 of Title 17

Limitations on exclusive rights: Reproduction by libraries and archives

(a) Except as otherwise provided in this title and notwithstanding the provisions of section 106, it is not an infringement of copyright for a library or archives, or any of its employees acting within the scope of their employment, to reproduce no more than one copy or phonorecord of a work, except as provided in subsections (b) and (c), or to distribute such copy or phonorecord, under the conditions specified by this section, if—

(1) the reproduction or distribution is made without any purpose of direct or indirect commercial advantage;

(2) the collections of the library or archives are (i) open to the public, or (ii) available not only to researchers affiliated with the library or archives or with the institution of which it is a part, but also to other persons doing research in a specialized field; and

(3) the reproduction or distribution of the work includes a notice of copyright that appears on the copy or phonorecord that is reproduced under the provisions of this section, or includes a legend stating that the work may be protected by copyright if no such notice can be found on the copy or phonorecord that is reproduced under the provisions of this section.

(151)

(b) The rights of reproduction and distribution under this section apply to three copies or phonorecords of an unpublished work duplicated solely for purposes of preservation and security or for deposit for research use in another library or archives of the type described by clause (2) of subsection (a), if—

(1) the copy or phonorecord reproduced is currently in the collections of the library or archives; and

(2) any such copy or phonorecord that is reproduced in digital format is not otherwise distributed in that format and is not made available to the public in that format outside the premises of the library or archives.

(c) The right of reproduction under this section applies to three copies or phonorecords of a published work duplicated solely for the purpose of replacement of a copy or phonorecord that is damaged, deteriorating, lost, or stolen, or if the existing format in which the work is stored has become obsolete, if—

(1) the library or archives has, after a reasonable effort, determined that an unused replacement cannot be obtained at a fair price; and

(2) any such copy or phonorecord that is reproduced in digital format is not made available to the public in that format outside the premises of the library or archives in lawful possession of such copy.

For purposes of this subsection, a format shall be considered obsolete if the machine or device necessary to render perceptible a work stored in that format is no longer manufactured or is no longer reasonably available in the commercial marketplace.

(d) The rights of reproduction and distribution under this section apply to a copy, made from the collection of a library or archives where the user makes his or her request or from that of another library or archives, of no more than one article or other contribution to a copyrighted collection or periodical issue, or to a copy or phonorecord of a small part of any other copyrighted work, if—

(1) the copy or phonorecord becomes the property of the user, and the library or archives has had no notice that the copy or phonorecord would be used for any purpose other than private study, scholarship, or research; and

(2) the library or archives displays prominently, at the place where orders are accepted, and includes on its order form, a warning of copyright in accordance with requirements that the Register of Copyrights shall prescribe by regulation.

(e) The rights of reproduction and distribution under this section apply to the entire work, or to a substantial part of it, made from the collection of a library or archives where the user makes his or her request or from that of another library or archives, if the library or archives has first determined, on the basis of a reasonable investigation, that a copy or phonorecord of the copyrighted work cannot be obtained at a fair price, if—

(1) the copy or phonorecord becomes the property of the user, and the library or archives has had no notice that the copy or phonorecord would be used for any purpose other than private study, scholarship, or research; and

(2) the library or archives displays prominently, at the place where orders are accepted, and includes on its order form, a warning of copyright in accordance with requirements that the Register of Copyrights shall prescribe by regulation.

(f) Nothing in this section—

(1) shall be construed to impose liability for copyright infringement upon a library or archives or its employees for the unsupervised use of reproducing

equipment located on its premises: Provided, That such equipment displays a notice that the making of a copy may be subject to the copyright law;

(2) excuses a person who uses such reproducing equipment or who requests a copy or phonorecord under subsection (d) from liability for copyright infringement for any such act, or for any later use of such copy or phonorecord, if it exceeds fair use as provided by section 107;

(3) shall be construed to limit the reproduction and distribution by lending of a limited number of copies and excerpts by a library or archives of an audiovisual news program, subject to clauses (1), (2), and (3) of subsection (a); or

(4) in any way affects the right of fair use as provided by section 107, or any contractual obligations assumed at any time by the library or archives when it obtained a copy or phonorecord of a work in its collections.

(g) The rights of reproduction and distribution under this section extend to the isolated and unrelated reproduction or distribution of a single copy or phonorecord of the same material on separate occasions, but do not extend to cases where the library or archives, or its employee:

153

(1) is aware or has substantial reason to believe that it is engaging in the related or concerted reproduction or distribution of multiple copies or phonorecords of the same material, whether made on one occasion or over a period of time, and whether intended for aggregate use by one or more individuals or for separate use by the individual members of a group; or

(2) engages in the systematic reproduction or distribution of single or multiple copies or phonorecords of material described in subsection (d): Provided, That nothing in this clause prevents a library or archives from participating in interlibrary arrangements that do not have, as their purpose or effect, that the library or archives receiving such copies or phonorecords for distribution does so in such aggregate quantities as to substitute for a subscription to or purchase of such work.

(h)

(1) For purposes of this section, during the last 20 years of any term of copyright of a published work, a library or archives, including a nonprofit educational institution that functions as such, may reproduce, distribute, display, or perform in facsimile or digital form a copy or phonorecord of such work,

or portions thereof, for purposes of preservation, scholarship, or research, if such library or archives has first determined, on the basis of a reasonable investigation, that none of the conditions set forth in subparagraphs (A), (B), and (C) of paragraph (2) apply.

(2) No reproduction, distribution, display, or performance is authorized under this subsection if—

    (A) the work is subject to normal commercial exploitation;

    (B) a copy or phonorecord of the work can be obtained at a reasonable price; or

    (C) the copyright owner or its agent provides notice pursuant to regulations promulgated by the Register of Copyrights that either of the conditions set forth in subparagraphs (A) and (B) applies.

(3) The exemption provided in this subsection does not apply to any subsequent uses by users other than such library or archives.

(i) The rights of reproduction and distribution under this section do not apply to a musical work, a pictorial, graphic or sculptural work, or a motion picture or other audiovisual work other than an audiovisual work dealing with news, except that no such limitation shall apply with respect to rights granted by subsections (b), (c), and (h), or with respect to pictorial or graphic works published as illustrations, diagrams, or similar adjuncts to works of which copies are reproduced or distributed in accordance with subsections (d) and (e). (U.S. Copyright Office, 2009)

The Digital Millennium Copyright Act (DCMA) of 1998 (selections)

Special Rules Regarding Liability of Nonprofit Educational Institutions Section 512(e) determines when the actions or knowledge of a faculty member or graduate student employee who is performing a teaching or research function may affect the eligibility of a nonprofit educational institution for one of the four limitations on liability. As to the limitations for transitory communications or system caching, the faculty member or student shall be considered a "person other than the provider," so as to avoid disqualifying the institution from eligibility. As to the other limitations, the knowledge or awareness of the faculty member or student will not be attributed to the institution. The following conditions must be met:

- the faculty member or graduate student's infringing activities do not involve providing online access to course materials that were required or recommended during the past three years;
- the institution has not received more than two notifications over the past three years that the faculty member or graduate student was infringing; and
- the institution provides all of its users with informational materials describing and promoting compliance with copyright law. (U.S. Copyright Office, 1998)

Distance Education Study

In the course of consideration of the DMCA, legislators expressed an interest in amending the Copyright Act to promote distance education, possibly through an expansion of the existing exception for instructional broadcasting in section 110(2). Section 403 of the DMCA directs the Copyright Office to consult with affected parties and make recommendations to Congress on how to promote distance education through digital technologies. The Office must report to Congress within six months of enactment.

The Copyright Office is directed to consider the following issues:

- The need for a new exemption;
- Categories of works to be included in any exemption;
- Appropriate quantitative limitations on the portions of works that may be used under any exemption;
- Which parties should be eligible for any exemption;
- Which parties should be eligible recipients of distance education material under any exemption;
- The extent to which use of technological protection measures should be mandated as a condition of eligibility for any exemption;
- The extent to which the availability of licenses should be considered in assessing eligibility for any exemption; and Other issues as appropriate. (U.S. Copyright Office, 1998)

Exemption for Nonprofit Libraries and Archives

Section 404 of the DMCA amends the exemption for nonprofit libraries and archives in section 108 of the Copyright Act to accommodate digital technologies and evolving preservation practices. Prior to enactment of the DMCA, section 108 permitted such libraries and archives to make a single facsimile (i.e., not digital) copy of a work for purposes of preservation or interlibrary loan. As amended, section 108 permits up to three copies, which may be digital, provided that digital copies are not made available to the public outside the library premises. In addition, the amended section permits such a library or archive to copy a work into a new format if the original format becomes obsolete—that is, the machine or device used to render the work perceptible is no longer manufactured or is no longer reasonably available in the commercial marketplace. (U.S. Copyright Office, 1998)

REFERENCES

U.S. Copyright Office. 1998. *The Digital Millennium Copyright Act of 1998*. U.S. Copyright Office. http://copyright.gov/legislation/hr2281.pdf.

U.S. Copyright Office. 2009. "U.S. Copyright Law." U.S. Copyright Office. www.copyright.gov/title17/.

U.S. House of Representatives. 2004. "The United States Constitution." U.S. House of Representatives. www.house.gov/house/Constitution/Constitution.html.

Appendix B

COUNTER Code of Practice
for Books and Reference Works: Release 1

Register of Vendors Providing Usage Reports Compliant with
Release 1 of the Code of Practice for Books and Reference Works

Last updated: March 2011

Vendor	Reports provided by Vendor						Reports available in XML?
	BR1	BR2	BR3	BR4	BR5	BR6	
ACS Publications		Yes			Yes		No
American Institute of Physics		Yes					Yes
Association for Computing Machinery	Yes						Yes
Atypon		Yes		Yes		Yes	No
Blackwell Publishing Ltd		Yes		Yes		Yes	Yes
Credo Reference (formerly XRefer)	Yes					Yes	No
Dawson Books Ltd	Yes	Yes				Yes	No
ebrary		Yes	Yes	Yes	Yes	Yes	No
Elsevier BV		Yes					No
Emerald Group Publishing Limited		Yes					No
Greenwood Publishing Group	Yes	Yes			Yes		No
HighWire Press		Yes				Yes	
IEEE Computer Society	Yes					Yes	No
Informa	Yes	Yes	Yes			Yes	No
Institute of Electrical and Electronics Engineers (IEEE)	Yes					Yes	No
Institute of Physics Publishing (IOPP)	Yes					Yes	No
Irish Newspapers Archives	Yes						
John Wiley & Sons Inc		Yes			Yes		No
Karger AG		Yes				Yes	Yes
Macmillan Publishing Solutions (MPS Insight)	Yes					Yes	No
MetaPress		Yes					No
MyiLibrary	Yes	Yes				Yes	No
Nature Publishing Group	Yes					Yes	No
Ovid Technologies	Yes		Yes	Yes		Yes	No
Oxford Scholarship Online		Yes	Yes		Yes		No
Palgrave Connect	Yes					Yes	No
Royal Society of Chemistry	Yes					Yes	No
Safari Books Online		Yes		Yes		Yes	No

Vendor	Reports provided by Vendor						Reports available in XML?
	BR1	BR2	BR3	BR4	BR5	BR6	
Sage Publications		Yes				Yes	No
Scholarly iQ	Yes	Yes					Yes
Scholar's Portal		Yes				Yes	Yes
SpringerLink		Yes					No
Thieme Publishing Group		Yes	Yes	Yes	Yes		No
Value Chain International	Yes					Yes	No
Wolters Kluwer Health Medical Research	Yes		Yes	Yes		Yes	Yes

BR2 = Book Report 2: Number of Successful Section Requests by Month and Title

BR3 = Book Report 3: Turnaways by Month and Title

BR4 = Book Report 4: Turnaways by Month and Service

BR5 = Book Report 5: Total Searches and Sessions by Month and Title

BR6 = Book Report 6: Total Searches and Sessions by Month and Service

Note: Full descriptions of the Usage Reports may be found, along with examples, in Section 4 of the COUNTER Code of Practice for Books and Reference Works. Vendors highlighted in red text [reproduced as italic] offer services to develop and support COUNTER compliant usage reports for other publishers.

Source: Reproduced by permission of COUNTER Online Metrics. Adapted to fit the format of this book.

Appendix C

COUNTER Code of Practice for Journals and Databases: Release 3

Register of Vendors Providing Usage Reports Compliant with
Release 3 of the Code of Practice for Journals and Databases

Last updated: March 2011

*From 1 September 2009 only Vendors and Usage Reports included in
this list may be regarded as being COUNTER compliant.*

Vendor	Reports provided by Vendor											
	JR1	JR1a	JR2	JR5	DB1	DB2	DB3	CR1	CR2	JB1	JR3	JR4
ACS Publications	Yes							Yes			Yes	Yes
Adam Matthew Digital					Yes							
AlphaMed Press	Yes	Yes						Yes			Yes	Yes
American Academy of Pediatrics	Yes	Yes						Yes			Yes	Yes
American Association for the Advancement of Science	Yes	Yes	Yes					Yes			Yes	Yes
American Association for Cancer Research	Yes	Yes						Yes			Yes	Yes
American Association for Clinical Chemistry	Yes	Yes						Yes			Yes	Yes
American Association for the Advancement of Science	Yes	Yes						Yes			Yes	Yes
American Association of Petroleum Geologists	Yes	Yes						Yes			Yes	Yes
American Cancer Society	Yes	Yes						Yes			Yes	Yes
American College of Cardiology	Yes	Yes						Yes			Yes	Yes
American College of Physicians	Yes	Yes						Yes			Yes	Yes
American Dental Association	Yes	Yes						Yes			Yes	Yes
American Diabetes Association	Yes	Yes						Yes			Yes	Yes
American Geophysical Union	Yes		Yes		Yes	Yes						
American Heart Association	Yes	Yes						Yes			Yes	Yes
American Institute of Physics	Yes	Yes		Yes	Yes		Yes	Yes	Yes		Yes	Yes
American Medical Association	Yes	Yes						Yes			Yes	Yes
American Physical Society	Yes	Yes						Yes			Yes	
American Physiological Society	Yes	Yes						Yes			Yes	Yes
American Psychiatric Publishing Inc.	Yes	Yes						Yes			Yes	Yes

Vendor	Reports provided by Vendor											
	JR1	JR1a	JR2	JR5	DB1	DB2	DB3	CR1	CR2	JB1	JR3	JR4
American Psychological Association	Yes				Yes			Yes	Yes			
American Society for Biochemistry and Molecular Biology	Yes	Yes						Yes			Yes	Yes
American Society for Investigative Pathology	Yes	Yes						Yes			Yes	Yes
American Society for Microbiology	Yes	Yes						Yes			Yes	Yes
American Society of Agronomy	Yes	Yes			Yes							
American Society of Clinical Oncology	Yes	Yes						Yes			Yes	Yes
American Society of Hematology	Yes	Yes						Yes			Yes	Yes
American Speech-Language-Hearing Association	Yes	Yes						Yes			Yes	Yes
American Thoracic Society	Yes	Yes						Yes			Yes	Yes
Association for Computing Machinery	Yes							Yes		Yes		Yes
ASTM	Yes			Yes				Yes			Yes	
Atypon (excluding Atypon Link)	Yes	Yes		Yes			Yes	Yes	Yes		Yes	
Begell House Inc.	Yes	Yes						Yes				
Bentham Science Publishers	Yes											
Berkeley Electronic Press	Yes							Yes				
BioOne	Yes	Yes						Yes				
Bioscientifica	Yes	Yes						Yes			Yes	Yes
British Institute of Radiology	Yes	Yes						Yes			Yes	Yes
British Medical Journal Publishing Group	Yes	Yes			Yes			Yes	Yes		Yes	Yes
CAB International					Yes		Yes					
Cambridge University Press	Yes	Yes						Yes				
CSA	Yes		Yes		Yes	Yes	Yes	Yes				
Chadwyck-Healey	Yes		Yes		Yes	Yes	Yes	Yes	Yes			

163

Vendor	Reports provided by Vendor											
	JR1	JR1a	JR2	JR5	DB1	DB2	DB3	CR1	CR2	JB1	JR3	JR4
Cold Spring Harbor Laboratory Press	Yes	Yes						Yes			Yes	Yes
Company of Biologists	Yes	Yes						Yes			Yes	Yes
CSIRO Publishing	Yes							Yes				
de Gruyter	Yes	Yes						Yes				
Dow Jones & Company Inc	Yes				Yes	Yes						
Duke University Press	Yes	Yes						Yes			Yes	Yes
EBSCO Publishing	Yes				Yes		Yes	Yes	Yes			
Elsevier-Engineering Village					Yes				Yes			
Elsevier -Science Direct	Yes	Yes					Yes	Yes				
Elsevier-Scopus							Yes		Yes			
Emerald Group Publishing	Yes	Yes			Yes		Yes	Yes	Yes		Yes	Yes
Endocrine Society	Yes	Yes						Yes			Yes	Yes
European Association for Cardio-Thoracic Surgery	Yes	Yes						Yes			Yes	Yes
FASEB	Yes	Yes						Yes			Yes	Yes
Gale Cengage Learning	Yes				Yes		Yes	Yes	Yes			
Geological Society of America	Yes	Yes						Yes			Yes	Yes
Geological Society of London	Yes	Yes						Yes			Yes	Yes
Gerontological Society of America	Yes	Yes						Yes			Yes	Yes
HighWire Press	Yes	Yes	Yes					Yes			Yes	Yes
H W Wilson	Yes				Yes	Yes	Yes	Yes	Yes			
IEEE Computer Society	Yes	Yes						Yes			Yes	Yes
IGI Global	Yes				Yes		Yes					
Illumina	Yes				Yes		Yes	Yes	Yes			
Informa Healthcare	Yes	Yes						Yes				
INFORMS	Yes	Yes						Yes			Yes	Yes
Ingenta Connect	Yes							Yes				
Institute of Electrical and Electronics Engineers (IEEE)	Yes	Yes						Yes			Yes	Yes

Vendor	Reports provided by Vendor											
	JR1	JR1a	JR2	JR5	DB1	DB2	DB3	CR1	CR2	JB1	JR3	JR4
Institute of Physics Publishing (IOPP)	Yes			Yes				Yes			Yes	
Irish Newspapers Archives					Yes							
ISSEL	Yes	Yes	Yes	Yes	Yes	Yes	Yes	Yes	Yes	Yes	Yes	Yes
Japan Science and Technology Agency	Yes	Yes										
John Wiley & Sons	Yes	Yes										
Johns Hopkins University- Project Muse	Yes				Yes		Yes					
Journal of Studies on Alcohol and Drugs	Yes				Yes							
JSTOR	Yes	Yes						Yes				
Karger AG	Yes	Yes						Yes				
Mary Ann Liebert	Yes	Yes						Yes				
M A Healthcare	Yes							Yes			Yes	Yes
Macmillan Publishing Solutions (MPS Insight)	Yes	Yes	Yes	Yes	Yes	Yes		Yes	Yes		Yes	Yes
MetaPress	Yes			Yes				Yes				
Mineralogical Society of America	Yes	Yes						Yes			Yes	Yes
Mineralogical Society of Great Britain and Ireland	Yes	Yes						Yes			Yes	Yes
Morningstar Investment Research Center					Yes				Yes			
National Academy of Sciences	Yes	Yes						Yes			Yes	Yes
Nature Publishing Group	Yes			Yes				Yes			Yes	Yes
NewsBank Inc.	Yes				Yes		Yes					
Nurimedia	Yes			Yes	Yes			Yes				
OCLC	Yes				Yes	Yes	Yes	Yes	Yes			
Optical Society of America	Yes				Yes			Yes	Yes			
OVID Technologies	Yes	Yes	Yes		Yes	Yes	Yes	Yes	Yes			
Oxford University Press	Yes	Yes						Yes				
Paleontological Society	Yes	Yes						Yes			Yes	Yes
Palgrave Macmillan	Yes			Yes				Yes			Yes	Yes
Perseé	Yes			Yes							Yes	Yes

Vendor	Reports provided by Vendor											
	JR1	JR1a	JR2	JR5	DB1	DB2	DB3	CR1	CR2	JB1	JR3	JR4
Philosophy Documentation Center	Yes	Yes										
Physician Postgraduate Press	Yes				Yes			Yes				
Physiological Society	Yes	Yes						Yes			Yes	Yes
Portland Press	Yes							Yes			Yes	
Project Euclid	Yes	Yes					Yes	Yes				
ProQuest	Yes	Yes	Yes		Yes		Yes	Yes	Yes		Yes	
Psychonomic Society Publications	Yes	Yes						Yes			Yes	Yes
Publishing Technology (IngentaConnect plus websites)	Yes							Yes				
Radiological Society of North America	Yes	Yes						Yes			Yes	Yes
RMIT Publishing	Yes				Yes	Yes	Yes	Yes	Yes			
Rockefeller University Press	Yes	Yes						Yes			Yes	Yes
Royal College of Psychiatrists	Yes	Yes						Yes			Yes	Yes
Royal Society	Yes	Yes						Yes			Yes	Yes
Royal Society of Chemistry	Yes			Yes				Yes			Yes	Yes
Royal Society of Medicine	Yes	Yes						Yes			Yes	Yes
SAE International	Yes	Yes						Yes			Yes	Yes
Sage Publications	Yes	Yes						Yes			Yes	Yes
Scholarly iQ	Yes	Yes	Yes	Yes	Yes	Yes	Yes	Yes	Yes	Yes	Yes	Yes
Scholar's Portal	Yes			Yes								
Seismological Society of America	Yes	Yes						Yes			Yes	Yes
Society for Endocrinology	Yes	Yes						Yes			Yes	Yes
Society for General Microbiology	Yes	Yes						Yes			Yes	Yes
Society for Neuroscience	Yes	Yes						Yes			Yes	Yes
Soil Science Society of America	Yes	Yes						Yes			Yes	Yes
Springer Verlag	Yes			Yes				Yes				
Springer Verlag (Springer Protocols)	Yes							Yes				

Vendor	Reports provided by Vendor											
	JR1	JR1a	JR2	JR5	DB1	DB2	DB3	CR1	CR2	JB1	JR3	JR4
Swets	Yes							Yes				
Symposium Journals	Yes							Yes				
Thieme Publishing Group	Yes			Yes				Yes				
Thomson Reuters					Yes	Yes	Yes		Yes			
University of Chicago Press	Yes	Yes						Yes				
University of Wisconsin Press	Yes	Yes						Yes			Yes	Yes
Wolters Kluwer Health Medical Research	Yes	Yes	Yes		Yes	Yes	Yes	Yes	Yes			Yes

JR1 = Journal Report 1: Number of Successful Full-Text Article Requests by Month and Journal

JR1a = Journal Report 1a: Number of Successful Full-Text Article Requests from an Archive by Month and Journal

JR2 = Journal Report 2: Turnaways by Month and Journal

JR5 = Journal Report 5: Number of Successful Full-Text Article Requests by Year-of-Publication and Journal

DB1 = Database Report 1: Total Searches and Sessions by Month and Database

DB2 = Database Report 2: Turnaways by Month and Database

DB3 = Database Report 3: Total Searches and Sessions by Month and Service

CR1 = Consortium Report 1: Number of Successful Full-Text Journal Article or Book Chapter Requests by Month (XML only)

CR2 = Consortium Report 2: Total Searches by Month and Database (XML only)

JB1 = Journal/Book Report 1: Number of Full-Text item Requests by Month and Title (XML only) - *optional*

JR3 = Journal Report 3: Number of Successful Item Requests and Turnaways by Month, Journal and Page-Type - *optional*

JR4 = Journal Report 4: Total Searches Run by Month and Service - *optional*

Note: Vendors that provide a separately purchasable archive must provide either Journal Report 1a (JR1a) or Journal Report 5 (JR5). Vendors highlighted in red text [reproduced as italic] offer services to develop and support COUNTER compliant usage reports for other publishers.

Source: Reproduced by permission of COUNTER Online Metrics. Adapted to fit the format of this book.

About the Editor and Contributors

Ryan O. Weir, editor, is Assistant Professor, Director of Technical Services and Electronic Resources, for Murray State University in Murray, Kentucky. He received his master's from Indiana University SLIS Indianapolis in 2008. Ryan started his career in electronic resources as a staff member before graduating with his masters. While Ryan now manages the technical services unit for University Libraries, he has maintained the responsibilities of electronic resources librarian for his institution. He is interested in finding ways to help the library community and the community of vendors and publishers to increase effective and fruitful communication about resources and services. He believes that strengthening these relationships will be vital to the continued success of both organizations.

Regina Koury is Electronic Resources Librarian at Idaho State University. She previously worked at the University of Southern California, where she gained experience in electronic resources, print serials, interlibrary loan, and public desk services. Regina received a MLIS from the University of Pittsburgh and is currently working on her MEd in Instructional Technology at Idaho State University. She is active in local and national library associations, and her research interests include all aspects of electronic resource management.

Denise Pan, since 2008, supports student, faculty, and staff success in the role of Associate Director of Technical Services at the Auraria Library. This tri-institutional academic library serves the missions of the University of Colorado Denver, Metropolitan State College of Denver, and Community College of Denver. Pan originally concentrated on improving the access and discovery of online learning materials as Electronic Resources & Serials Librarian. Since her promotion to Associate Director of Technical Services, Pan facilitates the work flow processes between acquisitions, cataloging, and electronic resources. Her research has focused on enhancing infrastructure and improving work flow processes through technology and organizational management theories. She has an MA in history from the University of Colorado Boulder and an MLIS from San Jose State University.

George Stachokas is Electronic Resources Librarian at the Cunningham Memorial Library of Indiana State University. His unit implemented their library's first ERM, replaced all of their other e-resource management tools, redesigned webpages, and used a new classification system for free resources to improve search and discovery at ISU. He holds an MLIS degree from the University of Illinois at Urbana-Champaign and a Master of Arts in History from Indiana State University.

Geoffrey Timms is Assistant Professor and Electronic Resources and Web Services Librarian at Mercer University in Macon, Georgia. He received his MLIS degree from the University of South Carolina in 2006. Working in library systems, Timms is responsible for the management of electronic resources and for the maintenance and enhancement of the platforms through which those resources are delivered and discovered. Serving as a subject liaison to the sciences, Timms also experiences electronic resources from the public services perspective, enhancing his appreciation of the electronic resources life cycle from multiple angles. Timms is particularly interested in developing user-centric library websites, including the promotion of electronic resources relevant to the user's current course load.

Index